Drawing
Solutions

Drawing
Solutions
Albany Wiseman

COLLINS & BROWN

First published in Great Britain in 2002 by
Collins & Brown Limited
64 Brewery Road
London N7 9NT
A member of Chrysalis Books plc

Distributed in the United States and Canada by
Sterling Publishing Co, 387 Park Avenue South,
New York, NY 10016, USA

9 8 7 6 5 4 3 2 1

British Library Cataloguing-in-Publication Data:
A catalogue record for this book is available from the
British Library.

ISBN 1 84340 004 9 (HB)

Conceived, edited and designed by Collins & Brown Limited
Editorial Director: Roger Bristow
Project Editor: Katie Hardwicke
Design Manager: Liz Wiffen
Design: Grade Design Consultants, London
Photographer: Ben Wray

Reproduction by Classicscan Pte Ltd, Singapore
Printed and bound by Craft Print International Ltd, Singapore

Contents

Introduction

Any creative activity needs concentration and patience, and drawing and painting is a constant journey of discovery. This book has at times been a learning curve for me, even though I have made my living as an artist for many years. A few of the techniques were new to me, and I had great pleasure in discovering the mysteries of the likes of frottage (see Question 46), monoprints (see Question 48) and silverpoint drawing (see Question 31). I hope that the reader will share the same sense of discovery and be inspired to expand his or her repertoire of drawing techniques, styles and media.

The book grew into a drawing glossary, and led to me searching through a large amount of my work, some going back many years, occasionally eliciting a trip down memory lane. One hundred and one questions was quite a challenge, and some of the answers are necessarily abridged due to the pressure of space – subjects such as perspective and anatomy can only be touched upon. It is hoped that the reader will enjoy searching for further information in specialist books, or on the internet. Included in each chapter are simple step-by-step exercises, which show how to work with particular media or apply a certain technique in straightforward stages. I hope that they will help and encourage you to produce your own versions.

A book can only tell us so much – the joy comes from picking up a pencil, or pen and paper and just drawing. Observation is the key, the detail on a building, the rhythm of a figure walking, standing or sitting, the shape of a tree, leaf or flower, all extend our knowledge of 'seeing' and improving our drawing skills and visual memory. The more you draw, the more your confidence grows.

Keeping a sketchbook is a wonderful way to record and improve your skills, and can be used as reference for further work or just as a private journal. I have found that many of my own sketchbooks have not only been useful in finding images for this book, some recall a moment or a place more evocatively than a photograph.

Enjoy your journey.

Albany Wiseman

Chapter 1: Drawing Tools

A visit to your local art supply store will reveal an overwhelming display of drawing materials. The choice will suit every style and budget – from the humble pencil to coloured brush pens and flamboyant quills. It is worth having a selection of drawing tools to hand – try different media now and again to keep your drawings fresh.

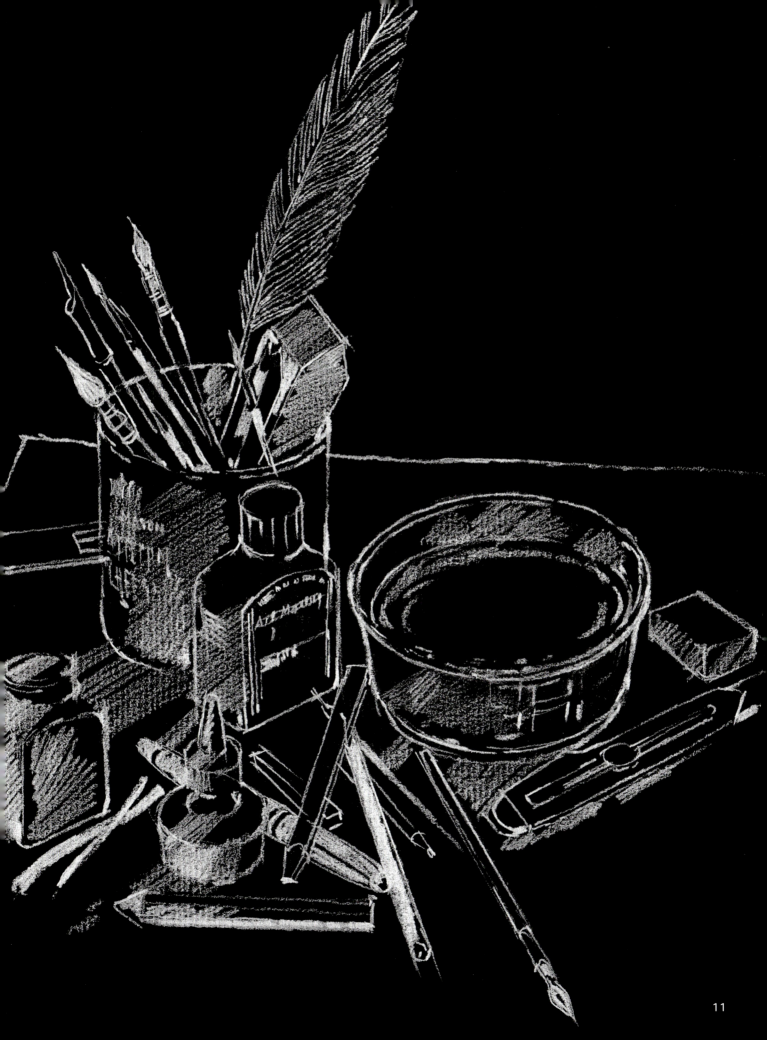

Q1 What equipment do I need to start drawing?

A | **The graphite pencil is the simplest and most readily available drawing tool.** It is inexpensive and very adaptable, and together with a good drawing paper or sketchbook, preferably cartridge paper, and an eraser and sharpener, you will have all that you need to start drawing.

There are many different grades of pencil (see Question 4), but an HB is ideal for simple sketches. Drawing media range from the humble pencil to coloured pencils, Conté pastels, fibre-tip pens, charcoal and fountain pens. Your choice of medium may be determined by your subject matter, but in the end it is often your personal style and preference that will guide you. The range of media, papers and drawing techniques will be explored in the following questions.

A pencil and eraser, together with a sketchbook or sheet of paper, are all that you need to start drawing.

This simple sketch was rendered in 4B pencil using loose shading marks. By changing the direction of the marks and varying the pressure applied with the pencil you can achieve a surprising range of tones with just one medium.

Q2 What equipment do I need for sketching?

A | **Sketches can be used as an aid to planning your composition, making notes on location, or as finished drawings in their own right.** Sketches can of course be made in any media – pencils, coloured pencils, ballpoint pens, brush pens and charcoal are all suitable for laying down quick, fluid lines. Choose a paper or sketchbook with a relatively smooth surface so that the pen or pencil will glide across the paper quickly.

A simple kit for sketching on location could include HB, 2B and 4B pencils, and a few coloured pencils that will enable you to take colour notes or complete a drawing in the field. Water-soluble coloured pencils will require a brush and a supply of water, but you can spread the colour in an arbitrary way by smudging with a wetted finger if necessary. A fountain pen and pocket-size sketchbook are ideal for spontaneous sketching on location.

Keep your equipment to a minimum – a lightweight bag and stool, a sketchbook or paper clipped to a board, eraser, pencils and pencil sharpener are all the basics you need.

Q3 What sort of sketchbook should I use?

A | **Since the advent of the 'Grand Tour' in the eighteenth century, artists have carried sketchbooks to record their travels.** A sketchbook is an invaluable part of your drawing kit, enabling you to experiment, doodle and gain confidence in your drawing skills.

There is an overwhelming variety of sketchbooks available. Before you make a purchase consider the size, the paper and the binding. Small pocket-size sketchbooks are easily carried and invaluable for making discreet drawings. A larger format may be more suited to landscape sketches or figure drawings. Smooth paper is suited to pencil, coloured pencil and pen and ink sketches, whereas you may require a paper with more 'tooth' or texture if you are drawing in charcoal or pastel.

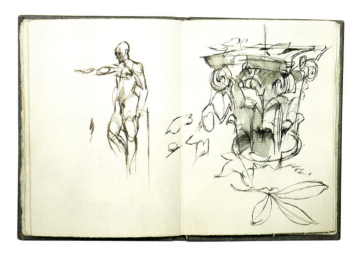

Sketchbooks with hard bindings provide protection for your drawings. Fill your sketchbooks with different subjects in a range of media and they will quickly become an invaluable source of reference.

Sketchbooks are available in different sizes and in different types of paper. Spiral-bound books can be opened flat and the pages easily removed if required.

Q4 What are the different grades of pencil used for?

A | **Graphite pencils are graded according to the density of the lead.** They are available in hard, medium or soft grades. There are over 21 grades, ranging from the very hard (9H) through to soft (9B). HB (hard black) is a medium lead in the middle of the range. HB to 6B are the most frequently used for drawing.

The harder H grades give a defined, grey line and are ideal for detailed, fine work. The softer B grades give a wide, black line. They are good for loose sketches or figure drawings. An HB or B pencil can be used for a range of purposes, from sketching to underdrawings for watercolour painting. A small selection of pencils, such as HB, 2B and 4B, will give you a range of tones and marks.

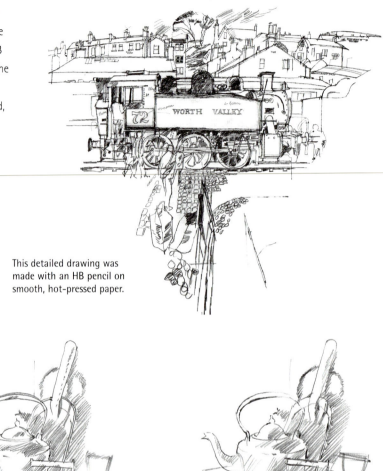

9H

HB

2B

4B

6B

7B

This detailed drawing was made with an HB pencil on smooth, hot-pressed paper.

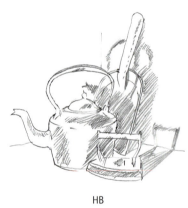

HB

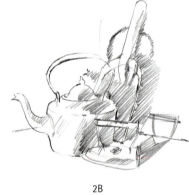

2B

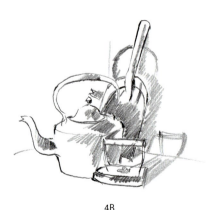

4B

7B

9B

14

Q5 What paper should I use for pencil drawing?

A | **There are many types of paper (support) that are ideal for pencil drawing.** The surface of the paper will affect the types of marks that you make. A smooth paper, such as hot-pressed, is good for fine, detailed work, whereas a textured paper, such as NOT or cold-pressed, is more suited to softer pencils and looser lines. Ingres, used for pastel drawing, has fine 'laid' lines that add texture to pencil marks. Cartridge, or drawing paper, that is neither too rough nor too smooth is a good all-purpose surface for pencil drawings and is readily available in loose sheets or in sketchbooks. Acid-free paper will stand the ravages of time without yellowing.

This scene of a French vineyard was made on a rough watercolour paper with a 4B pencil. The texture of the paper shows through the broad pencil marks and enhances the tonal range.

I used smooth cartridge or drawing paper for this quick portrait sketch. Fluid lines and loose shading can be quickly laid down on a smooth paper.

Q6 What is a suitable paper for charcoal drawing?

A | **Charcoal was one the earliest materials for making marks.** It is very black and soft and requires a paper with texture or 'tooth' to hold the powder to the surface, although you can work successfully on a smooth paper.

Ingres papers, named after the French Neo-Classical painter Jean-Auguste Dominique Ingres (1780–1867), have laid lines and are available in gentle tones that are ideal for charcoal. The rough side of ordinary 'kraft' or brown wrapping paper will also take charcoal well, as do the Indian 'Khadi' rag papers. Consider a coloured or toned paper for your charcoal drawing. A midtone will reduce the harsh contrast of black on white and will enable you to add a different dimension to your drawing. Sugar paper is inexpensive and is available in a range of colours.

Use an aerosol fixative or hairspray to fix your charcoal drawing to prevent it from smudging (see Question 15).

A toned Ingres paper provides a unifying background for a more detailed figure study. The textured surface holds the charcoal, which can then be smudged and blended to vary the depth of tone.

A simple charcoal outline drawing works well on smooth cartridge or drawing paper.

Q7 What is a suitable paper for pastel drawing?

A | Pastel is another soft medium, similar to charcoal, and it requires a paper with texture or tooth in order for the powder to adhere to the surface. Pastel papers are available in a range of colours that can provide a unifying background for your subject. Select a colour that complements your subject matter or that provides a neutral midtone from which to work (see Question 21).

The following papers are ideal for pastel drawings: Ingres is available in a range of colours that give you a toned ground; the Canson range is reasonably inexpensive and available in a variety of weights and colours; Sansfix is a rough-textured paper that does not need fixing; velours or flock papers give a dramatic light and shade effect; sandgrain paper is suited to strong, bold drawings, but it will wear the pastel away quickly; sugar paper is available in a range of colours.

You will need to fix your drawing with aerosol fixative or hairspray to prevent it from smudging. An alternative method is to hold the drawing over steam from a boiling kettle. This will melt the pigment slightly.

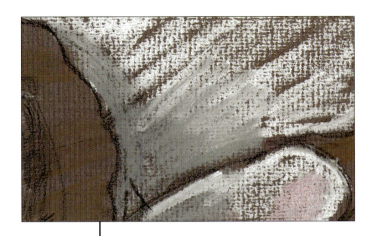

Light marks of white pastel show the grain of the underlying paper

This preliminary pastel sketch was made on a dark Ingres paper. The rough surface holds the pastel powder and solid marks can be applied to vary the depth of colour.

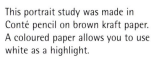

This portrait study was made in Conté pencil on brown kraft paper. A coloured paper allows you to use white as a highlight.

Blue sugar paper is an inexpensive choice for pastel drawings. It has a lightly textured surface that suits soft pastels.

This standing figure was drawn on a smooth sheet of board. The pastel was smudged with my finger to solidify the tone along the leg.

Q8 What is a suitable paper for pen and ink drawings?

A | A smooth paper is ideal for ink drawings, allowing the pen to glide across the surface, giving a fluid, unbroken line. Smooth hot-pressed papers, such as Bristol paper or Schöllershammer, work well and allow you the flexibility of scratching out mistakes without the paper furring. These papers are good for dip pens or fountain pens. Cartridge or drawing paper varies in thickness and quality and is suitable for fountain pens and technical pens. A semi-rough Ingres paper or rough cartridge paper can be used to give a 'broken' line.

This sketch was made with a fountain pen in a small sketchbook. You can achieve a range of marks with dashed lines and loose hatching.

This detailed drawing was made with a dip pen on a hard, smooth paper. The clean lines are ideally suited to the linear qualities of the boat and building.

Q9 What pens should I use for ink drawings?

A | As much as everyone has an individual drawing style, there are pens to match. There is no ideal pen to use for ink drawings, although the traditional steel nibs are the most common. They are available in many different styles and may have interchangeable nibs, giving you the choice of rounded, square or pointed tips. Sketching pens are also available, as are bamboo pens.

Technical pens, such as those used in architectural drawings, have a standard-sized tip that produces a uniform line. Readily-available writing pens, such as ballpoint or fibre-tip pens (see Question 28), can also be used to good effect.

When selecting a pen, try out a few strokes so that you are aware of the different marks that each type produces. Use a variety of papers to experiment on, as the surface will also affect the texture of the mark. Choose between pens that need a separate ink supply or those with an ink reservoir.

Dip pen
The size of the nib can be changed to produce lines of varying thickness.

Felt- or fibre-tip pen
There are many varieties available in different thicknesses and colours. The line is even and mechanical.

Fountain pen
You can draw a 'free' line and vary the width of the mark by turning the pen to use the back of the nib.

Reed pen
These pens produce short, thick strokes and a soft line.

Quill pen
These pens produce smooth, fluid marks.

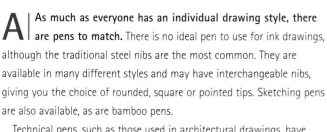

This street scene in a French village was drawn using a dip pen and waterproof ink. You can achieve thick and thin lines by varying the pressure of the mark or by changing the nib.

Q10 Can I make my own pens?

A | **It is possible to follow the traditional methods of the early artists and make your own ink pens from either a reed or quill.** Before the advent of steel nibs, pens were cut to shape using a 'pen' knife. Goose or turkey wing feathers are strong and stout and can be easily cut. Depending on the way the 'nib' is cut, you can vary the type of line produced from positive, sweeping strokes to thin, delicate marks. A blunt, chisel-cut nib will give you broad strokes, or by shaping the nib to a point you can make a thin line. Bamboo and reeds can also be cut in the same way and will give a strong, bold line. The use of sepia coloured ink suits a quill pen and gives an authentic look to sketches and figure studies, reminiscent of the Old Masters.

Simple hatching and outline drawing are effectively combined in this portrait drawn with a quill pen using sepia ink on a lightly toned paper.

This quick sketch of trees was made with a reed pen and waterproof ink. The broad strokes lend themselves to linear subjects.

Project

MATERIALS   Goose feather, scalpel or sharp knife

Feathers are available from art stores. Choose a large, strong feather, as
weaker feathers may split when shaping the nib.

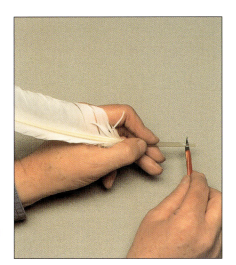

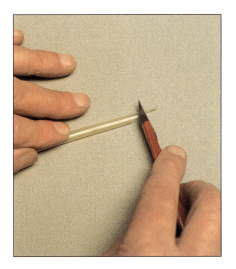

1 Use a scalpel or sharp knife to trim any
loose skin and barbs away from the base of
the feather. Rest the feather on a hard surface
and scrape away about 3 in (7.5 cm) above the tip
with the knife facing away from your body. **Inset:**
Using the scalpel or sharp knife, make a diagonal
cut across the tip of the feather.

2 Place the feather on a hard surface and cut
a scoop from the underside 1 in (2.5 cm)
from the tip halfway through the stem. If the
quill contains keratin, scrape it out carefully
with a knife.

3 Using the scalpel or sharp knife, make a
small slit in the centre of the quill. Extend
the slit by carefully pushing up from underneath
with a knife handle or another quill.

4 Shape the nib to a point with the scalpel.
If the nib is thick, make a chisel-shaped tip
by cutting the very tip of the quill diagonally
downwards. Rub the nib with sandpaper to
smooth any rough edges.

Q11 What is waterproof ink?

A | Waterproof Indian ink (or Chinese ink) is shellac-based and enables washes to be applied over a drawing without the ink **running.** Waterproof inks are available in a range of colours, and also as liquid acrylic inks. There is a good-range of fibre-tip pens available that are waterproof. Check the solubility of the ink before buying. Waterproof ink is unsuitable for fountain pens as it clogs the pen. There are black inks available that are non-clogging, although these are not completely waterproof. Calligraphy ink can be used in a fountain pen. Black Indian ink can thicken with age, so add a few drops of distilled water to help the ink flow.

Short strokes of different coloured inks were overlaid to build up the texture of the cabbage leaves

For this leaf study I used a sepia coloured waterproof ink and applied a watercolour wash on the top once the ink had dried.

This still life sketch uses different coloured inks. One advantage of using waterproof inks is that you can layer colours without the risk of the inks running.

Q12 What is water-soluble ink?

A | **Water-soluble inks can be diluted with water to achieve half-tones and washes.** Ink used in fountain or dip pens, such as black, blue/black, sepia, green and blue, have no added shellac so will spread if water is applied. The effect can enhance a drawing by softening lines and blurring the image. Chinese sticks of ink are available in a range of colours, together with black. By rubbing the stick in a small palette with distilled water, very deep black or coloured ink can be made. There are water-soluble fibre-tip and brush pens also available, which create a soft line when water is applied.

There are many different methods of working with water-soluble inks. You can use a damp brush to work over the ink line, softening it and spreading the ink to vary the tones. You can apply a wash of dilute ink over dried waterproof ink, and vary the dilutions of the ink wash to achieve a range of tones or colours. A slightly unpredictable technique is to draw on to damp paper (see below).

In this sketch, a wash of light ochre watercolour was applied over water-soluble ink. The slight variations in tone capture the texture and warmth of the building's exterior plaster.

For this quick sketch I used a fountain pen on damp paper. Fine, clean lines appeared where the paper was relatively dry, and blurred lines where the ink bled into the damp patches.

23

Q13 What is a mirror used for?

A| When we draw on a horizontal board or pad of paper, rather than on a vertical easel, our head, hands and eyes are not immediately above the drawing, resulting in distortion. A mirror, held up at eye level to reflect the drawing, can be used to check for any inaccuracies, such as an elongated arm in a figure drawing or incorrect perspective in a landscape or still life. Another simple way of checking when using a lightweight paper is to hold the drawing up to the light and looking at it from the reverse side. It is remarkable how any inaccuracies will leap out at you.

Portrait and figure studies need to be checked regularly to ensure that the balance of features and proportions are correct. Hold a small mirror next to your drawing and look carefully at the reflection.

Q14 How do I use a viewfinder?

A | **A viewfinder, simply made from a piece of card, or two 'Ls', preferably in a neutral colour, will help you to frame your subject matter and select your composition.** It can be used indoors, for example, to establish the parameters and shape of a still life, or by holding it in various positions near and away from you outdoors to choose the balance and composition of a landscape picture. By holding the viewfinder close to your eye the picture area becomes larger, whereas by holding it further away you crop in on the picture space, making for a tighter, more controlled image. The viewfinder gives you the option of a portrait or landscape format. It is worth spending some time to establish your picture area – we often see too much and the viewfinder helps to eliminate distracting detail and to select the main elements of the picture.

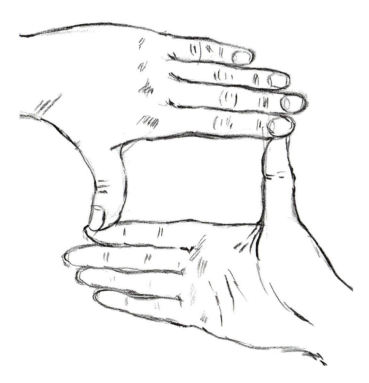

The 'film director's' viewfinder seen through your hands is a convenient alternative if you don't have a card version available.

Frame your subject through the viewfinder. This portrait format suits the tall vase of flowers. By bringing the viewfinder closer to your face you can change the crop to include more background detail.

Q15 How do I prevent my drawings from smudging?

A | Soft drawing materials, such as charcoal, pastel and the soft 6B, 7B and 8B pencils, will smudge if rubbed. A fixative should be used to protect your finished pastel and charcoal drawings, such as aerosol fixative spray, hairspray or steam from a boiling kettle. It is also advisable to fix your drawing at regular intervals as you work. A wash of clean water applied on top of a graphite drawing will also help to fix the image, although thin paper may cockle. A thin detail paper is available for protecting drawings, and some pastel sketchbooks are interleaved with protective sheets between the pages.

Your drawing may smudge as your hand moves across it – a piece of scrap paper beneath your hand will help to protect the drawing as you work. Sometimes intentional smudging is a bonus and a useful technique for softening lines and adding tone. You can use your finger or a tortillon (see below) to smudge lines intentionally.

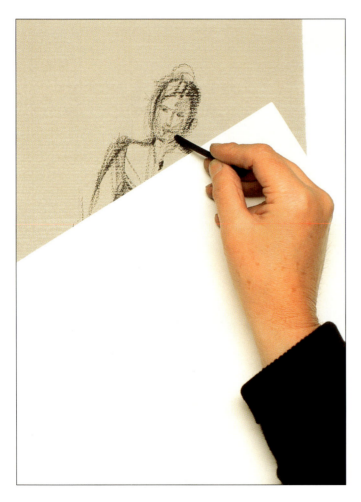

Place a clean sheet of paper over the lower half of the drawing. The paper will prevent your hand from smudging the underlying drawing.

You can use a soft kneaded eraser or tortillon to lift-off highlights and draw into the charcoal, smudging the lines intentionally.

Q16 How do I keep my pencils sharp?

A | **A sharp or shaped pencil tip is essential.** There are several ways of sharpening pencils: a craft knife will give a good point facing away from your body, cut a generous amount of wood, leaving a good point to the lead, you can then use the side of the lead for shading, and the tip for finer details. A chisel-shaped pencil tip can be made and maintained by sharpening with a craft knife; the resulting line will be thick and bold. You can use the side of the point for shading and the sharp tip for detail.

Alternatively, a sandpaper block is useful for keeping a sharp point. Pencil sharpeners are practical but can sometimes break a soft lead and do not give you any control over the shape of the tip. Bear in mind that a rough paper will quickly wear down a soft lead.

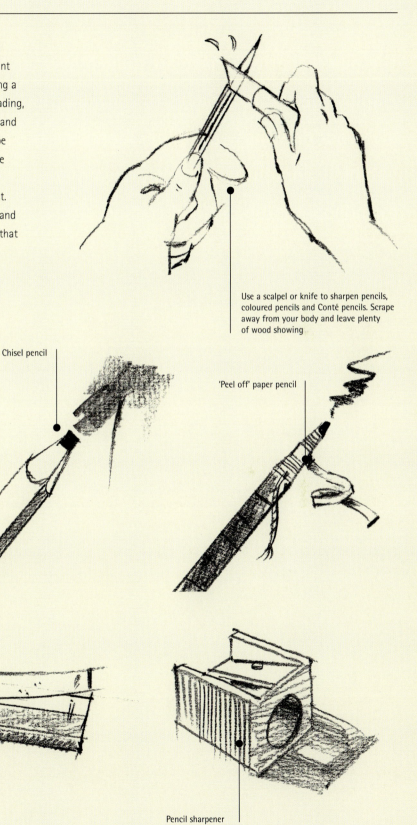

Use a scalpel or knife to sharpen pencils, coloured pencils and Conté pencils. Scrape away from your body and leave plenty of wood showing

Long, sharp point

Chisel pencil

'Peel off' paper pencil

Sandpaper block

Pencil sharpener

Chapter 2 Drawing Techniques

The marks that you make are guided by your own drawing style, but you can employ specific techniques to convey different effects, textures and tones to give your drawings added life. Alongside the artist's standard techniques of hatching, contour and shade drawing are the more unusual effects produced by monoprints, stipple and collage.

Q17 Can I use different pencil grades in the same drawing?

A The range of marks available from the different pencil grades makes them ideal for tonal drawing, working from the darkest soft B grades to the lighter hard H grades. Using the light and dark tones will give your drawing added depth. In landscape drawing particularly, objects are lighter in the distance, an effect known as aerial perspective (see Question 65), and you can render this effectively by combining hard and soft grades in the same drawing.

This drawing uses three pencil grades: 8B, B and HB. The wide range of tones is achieved by varying the pressure of the marks.

The midtones of the middle ground posts were drawn with HB and B pencils

The light tones of the distant hills were drawn with an HB pencil

The dark tones in the foreground were drawn with an 8B pencil

Q18 How do I draw with coloured pencils?

A | **There are several kinds of coloured pencil – water-soluble, non-soluble and Conté.** You can achieve interesting effects with water-soluble pencils by adding water to make a wash or using a wetted finger to smudge and blend on the paper. Non-soluble and Conté pencils lend themselves to a variety of subjects; Conté pencils are suitable for figure drawing and are very effective on an Ingres coloured paper.

Tones can be gradually built up by grading colours, starting light and then moving darker to achieve depth. A rough paper will give added 'sparkle' where the pigment catches on the raised area of the paper surface.

A beautiful box of coloured pencils can look seductive in an art store but by purchasing individually you can select your personal choice of colours and tints.

For this sketch I used water-soluble coloured pencils on a rough paper. I smudged the marks to create blurred, soft tones in the trees.

This drawing combines several different techniques that lend themselves to drawing in coloured pencils. I used water-soluble pencils and blended them with a brush on the rooftop and in the background trees. Loose, scribbled marks and overlaid, broken colours were combined to describe the texture in the foreground (see left).

Q19 How do I draw with charcoal?

A | Charcoal is made from burnt vine, beech or willow twigs and is available either in a natural stick form or as compressed sticks or pencils. It is easy to work with and gives a loose, flowing line. Choose different stick thicknesses to vary the width of the line, and use a thick stick to lay in solid areas of colour. A thin stick or pencil can be used to draw finer details. The powdery nature of charcoal requires a textured paper (see Question 6), although any paper surface can be used.

Charcoal is an expressive medium, ideally suited to quick sketches or figure studies as it moves swiftly over the paper. You can add tone by blending and smudging the powder with your finger or a tortillon (see Question 15), or lift out highlights with a kneaded eraser (see Question 22). You will need to fix your drawing once it is finished.

In this study I used charcoal sticks to draw the outline of the figure, and then smudged and blended the marks to describe the model's hair.

This simple still life uses outline drawing with a stick of charcoal, combined with soft tonal shading to describe the shapes and forms of the vegetables.

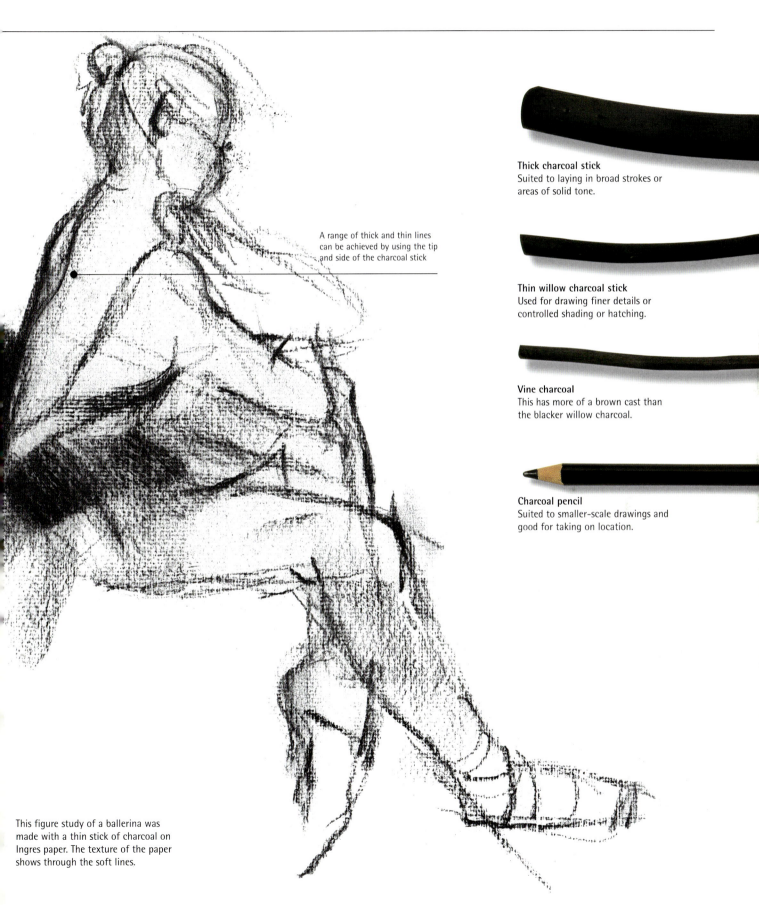

A range of thick and thin lines can be achieved by using the tip and side of the charcoal stick

This figure study of a ballerina was made with a thin stick of charcoal on Ingres paper. The texture of the paper shows through the soft lines.

Thick charcoal stick
Suited to laying in broad strokes or areas of solid tone.

Thin willow charcoal stick
Used for drawing finer details or controlled shading or hatching.

Vine charcoal
This has more of a brown cast than the blacker willow charcoal.

Charcoal pencil
Suited to smaller-scale drawings and good for taking on location.

Q20 What is a tonal drawing?

A | Tone is the lightness or darkness of a colour, judged on a scale between black and white. The use of tone or 'shading' expresses the light and dark areas of subjects, giving a third dimension and depth to the drawing. For example, an orange, just drawn as a circle, shows no solidity, but the addition of a light source will produce form and shadows. 'Local' colour – the actual colour of an object – will help the overall pattern and character of your drawing by introducing more tonal range.

Tone can be achieved by various grades of pencil and the strength and density of the marks. You can vary the density of the marks by turning the pencil or using drawing techniques such as hatching and cross-hatching (see Question 41).

Choose a smooth paper to achieve more solid, defined tone, and a rougher paper for more broken texture. A tonal drawing can be completed using pen and ink, pencils or pastels, but always work in monochrome.

Dense tone indicates the deep shadows of the pepper halves

Highlights were lifted out with a kneaded eraser

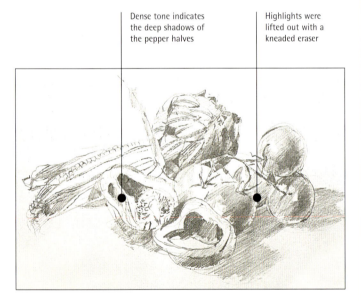

This simple still life uses a range of tones to describe the varied shapes of the vegetables. Different tones were achieved by using pencils with soft and hard leads and by varying the pressure of the marks.

The tonal range, from light to dark, was achieved with different grades of pencil.

HB

2B

4B

8B

Q21 What is a toned ground?

A | A toned ground is a coloured surface on which to draw; it provides the background for your work and will enhance a coloured or tonal drawing. A neutral midtone is ideal, as you can add lighter and darker tones to build up the image. A toned ground is practical for portraits or figure studies as it is less abrasive than a harsh white background and provides unity across the image. Different coloured papers are available, and you can select from the warm tones of light browns or pinks or the cooler tones of grey and blue. A toned ground gives you the opportunity to use white to add highlights. Always choose a middle tone that will contrast with white and show the darker tones.

You can make your own toned paper. For a soft brown, try wiping coffee or a damp tea bag across the paper in even strokes, suitable for pencil or ink drawings. Pastel, charcoal and graphite powder can also be used to make a toned ground – remember to fix them before drawing.

This portrait study was drawn on a mid-blue sugar paper with charcoal and white pastel for the highlights.

Q22 How do I 'draw' with an eraser?

A | An eraser can be used as another drawing tool on charcoal, pencil, graphite powder or pastel drawings, to lift off colour and add highlights to give form, texture and volume. Use an eraser to define highlights in figure drawings and still lifes – in landscapes it is invaluable for suggesting snow or mist. Think of it as working from dark to light, using the eraser to add highlights and create lighter tones. This technique works best on a smooth paper, as rough paper holds the pigment in the surface.

A soft kneaded eraser can be shaped to a point to enable you to 'draw' lines and finer details. Retractable erasers are available which give you the option of a pointed or flat side to produce different lines. They also keep your hand away from the paper and thus prevent smudging. Some plastic erasers can leave small pieces of rubber on your drawing; gently blow them away. A rolled piece of paper or tortillon is traditionally used for adding highlights to charcoal drawings.

In this sidelit study, broad marks of charcoal were smudged to create a solid tone out of which the highlights were lifted with an eraser. The strands of hair were 'drawn' with an eraser.

Project

MATERIALS   Graphite powder, soft kneaded eraser, retractable eraser, acid-free drawing paper

The impression of a cold, snow-covered landscape can be quickly achieved by using an eraser to draw into a prepared ground of graphite powder. Blow away any eraser debris – do not brush it, as this will smudge the powder.

1 Sprinkle the graphite powder onto the paper and rub in with your fingers. Spread the powder to establish your picture area, pressing harder to achieve a darker tone. For landscape images create a darker tone at the top of the paper. Keep applying the graphite powder until you have achieved the desired depth of tone.

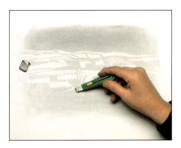

2 With a clean edge to the eraser, start to define the shapes of the distant hills and fields, starting with the horizon. Use a kneaded eraser to rub away large areas such as the fields. 'Draw' the trees, buildings and walls with the retractable eraser by simply rubbing away the graphite powder to reveal the paper beneath, which reads as snow.

Small details for roofs, windows and doors were drawn with the retractable eraser

3 Use the harder edge of the retractable eraser to outline the buildings, windows and chimneys. With broad strokes of the kneaded eraser, remove the powder in the foreground. Fix the image.

35

Q23 How do I draw with soft pastels?

A │ **Pastels are made from a dry colour pigment bound with gum into a stick form.** They are soft and powdery but give a rich, strong colour that can be blended and smudged. Pastel pencils, known as Conté pencils, are harder, easily managed and sharpened, and more practical for detailed work. They can be blended and mixed with broader strokes of soft pastels.

Strictly speaking, the use of pure pastel is defined as 'painting', but there are many techniques that also apply to drawing. Large round sticks of pastel can be used to lay broad areas of colour, and these can be combined with smaller, shorter strokes to build layers of colour. By laying dashes of different colours next to each other you can blend the colours in the viewer's eye – a technique known as broken colour. Alternatively, overlay colours and smudge with your finger to intensify the hue. Pastels lend themselves to scribbled marks and shading. You can work from dark to light, overlaying darker colours with lighter tones to suggest highlights. Apply the pastels with light strokes to begin with, then use firmer marks to intensify the colours and deepen the tones.

Choose a paper with a texture, such as Ingres paper, which will hold the powder pigment and fix your drawing as you work, to prevent smudging and keep the colours crisp (see Question 15).

Pastels lend themselves to a variety of subjects, but their qualities of intense colour are well suited to sunlit scenes or landscapes involving rippled water and reflections. The wonderful range of colours lend themselves very well to flower drawings, too. The ease with which you can apply the strokes of colour also appeals to figure artists and portraitists.

The texture of Sansfix paper is ideal for blending and smudging colours. Here, loose strokes of colour have been overlaid to build up tone and depth.

In this study on a toned background, the broad strokes of pastel have been smudged to soften the tones and colours.

Project

MATERIALS   Soft pastels in a range of colours, Fabriano Roma paper, aerosol fixative spray

A flower study is an ideal subject for a pastel drawing. Select a coloured paper to act as a midtone to help to unify the colours and throw the image forward. Green is a good choice for arrangements with strong foliage, but a mid-blue or light brown would also be suitable.

1 Choose a light colour pastel to establish the composition. Loosely draw the simple shapes to establish the scale of the image and the balance of the different elements. Use an ellipse for the top and base of the vase and to represent the centre of the flowers where they are turned away from view.

2 Once the rough outline of the subject is complete, you can start to suggest and position further details, such as the leaves. With a light green, indicate the shapes of the leaves and stalks. Look for the negative shapes (see Question 59) to define the edges. When working with pastel you can work from dark to light, so use a darker green to suggest form.

3 Start to add detail to the vase to suggest form. Overlay light strokes of yellows, oranges and ochres to build up the colour. Use a darker tone on the shadowed side and add bright highlights. **Inset:** Working from dark to light, continue to build up the colours on the vase, blending the pastel on the paper surface. The shadow on the left establishes the light source.

4 Return to the flowers. Use a cool grey over the white of the petals to draw their shape – this tones down the stark white and establishes form. Use a brighter white on the edges, pressing firmly to give a more solid mark. Leave the paper to show through in some areas as a midtone. Add a light touch of bright green to the centre of the flowers and to the leaves.

5 To set the image in context add a background colour around and behind the vase. Use loose shading with harder edges around the vase to define its shape. Fill in the spaces between the leaves and flowers, using the negative shapes. The shadowed side should be darker – blend two colours together, rubbing with your finger to increase the depth of colour.

6 Continue to define the flowers, leaves and edge of the vase, and use a darker green or brown in the inner rim to suggest shadow. Add a mid-green to the leaves to define the shape further. Fix the image with aerosol fixative spray. When dry, add a dash of orange to the centre of the flowers. If the colour is too bright, knock it back with a touch of yellow on top.

Q24 How do I draw with oil pastels?

A Oil pastels have a translucent quality and are available in a wide range of vibrant colours. They are stronger than soft pastels, allowing broader, more positive marks to be made. Blending is more difficult than with soft pastels, and it is not possible to overlay colours as the marks become opaque when blended, although you can layer colours one on top of another so that the lower layer shows through. The antipathy of grease and water means that oil pastels can be used as a resist (see Question 27), giving you a broader range of techniques and effects. Sgraffito (see Question 33) is another technique that works well with oil pastel. Chinagraph or lithographic pencils can be used in conjunction with oil pastels to make drawing easier. You can work on any type of paper with oil pastels, although a rough paper will give a textured effect.

Because of their nature, oil pastels are suited to quick drawings and sketches and can be effective in abstract works where solid blocks of colour are required. The ease with which the pastel moves over the paper lends itself to contour drawing (see Question 40) and figure subjects.

The rich, vibrant colours of oil pastels lend themselves to studies of hot landscapes. This drawing uses a variety of different techniques to capture the textures of the scene.

Solid marks of colour give an intensity and depth to the bushes in the middle ground

Short strokes of overlaid colours represent the scrubby grass in the foreground

Sgraffito was used to give the effect of thin stalks of grass

Q25 When should I use line and wash?

A | **A wash is a useful way of introducing colour and soft tone into your drawing.** Drawings made solely with a pen or pencil rely on scribbled, hatched or cross-hatched marks to suggest tone and form. A colour wash, either added as an underlying tone or used to add 'local' colour, gives you more flexibility to enhance and add depth to your drawing. Ink washes also work well in monochrome for tonal drawings.

A wash can be made from watercolour paint, water-soluble ink, water-soluble coloured pencils and Indian ink. A smooth paper, such as cartridge or drawing paper, is ideal for line and wash drawings.

I drew this scene on location with a fountain pen and blue-black ink and added the watercolour washes later.

Project

MATERIALS Fountain pen, drawing paper, Chinese brush, water

A fountain pen with water-soluble ink and a damp brush are all you need for a quick line and wash sketch.

1 Sketch the outline of the cat, using fluid strokes and contour lines (see Question 40) to describe the shape and form. Cats can be simplified to a series of circles or ovals to describe their outline.

2 With a damp brush, follow the lines of the drawing. You can extend the wash with the brush to draw further details and add form. Here, I used the damp wash to follow the form of the cat's haunch and fill in the tail.

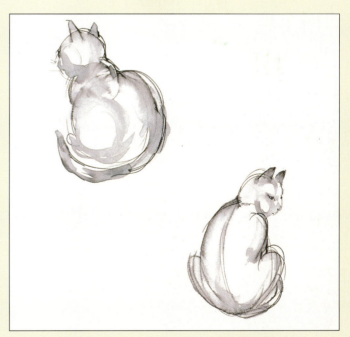

3 Once the wash has dried you can add further details of the eyes and mouth with the pen.

For this sketchbook study I used a 7B pencil and then added a wash of coffee on top. When on location, use whatever materials come to hand!

Q26 What is the 'spatter' technique?

A| Spattering is the effect created by flicking ink or paint across a drawing or painting, producing spots of ink that add texture and sparkle to the marks on the paper. It needs a little practise and experiment to master the effect.

There are several ways to spatter ink onto your drawing. Load a small brush with ink, hold it over the drawing and gently tap the brush onto your finger or another brush. Another method is to dip a toothbrush into ink and then rub the toothbrush with a matchstick, drawing the matchstick towards your body so that the ink flicks away, onto the paper.

Spattering can be used to represent rain or snow, pebbles on a beach or in a stream, or speckled fruit in a still life.

For this drawing I used a dip pen with black waterproof ink and lightly tapped the pen to produce the spots in the foreground.

Q27 What are resist techniques?

A| A resist technique uses a barrier to separate the ink or paint from the paper surface, leaving the colour of the paper blank. You can 'draw' with the resist, using it as another drawing tool. Most resist techniques use the antipathy between wax and water – for example you can 'draw' with a wax candle and then use water-based ink to wash over the marks. The candle lines will remain clear. Another resist method is to use masking fluid. This is a liquid latex solution used for stopping out areas prior to applying water-soluble inks. It produces a barrier to the ink and can be rubbed away once the wash has dried to reveal the clean paper beneath. It can be used to define edges and represent white highlights – for example use it to mask out clouds or birds, ship's masts and window frames.

When using masking fluid there are one or two 'dos and don'ts' to bear in mind. Don't put your brush on the fluid before the masked areas are dry, as it will clog the hairs on the brush. Try not to use a brush to apply the masking fluid unless it has been dipped in washing-up liquid first – this makes it much easier to wash the brush afterwards. Alternatively, apply the fluid with a reed or bamboo pen, as the dried latex can easily be removed.

The clear lines of the window frames was achieved by first drawing with masking fluid

Masking fluid is invaluable for detailed architectural drawings. Here, the window frames were masked before applying the ink.

Q28 How do I draw with fibre-tip pens?

A Although fibre-tip pens can be unforgiving they are a useful tool for the artist, especially for quick, spontaneous sketches. They are a perfectly acceptable medium for a more finished drawing, too – their range of colours and thicknesses make them very versatile ,and they save carrying bottles of different coloured ink. Use fibre-tip pens as you would any drawing medium, but bear in mind that the marks are permanent and cannot be corrected. This quality can be an advantage, your first tentative marks searching for shapes and form are an essential part of the drawing process and add to the spontaneity of a sketch.

This page from my sketchbook was filled with sketches using a fibre-tip sepia pen.

Q29 How do I draw with technical pens?

A | **The technical pen was originally designed for architects, draughtsmen and engineers.** It has a thin tube through which the ink is supplied and needs to be held horizontally in order for the ink to flow. It gives an even, constant line, and there are several different nib widths available. The technical pen lends itself to fine, precise drawing and is ideal for architectural details and linear subjects. It is not suited to a looser, more sketchy style of drawing.

Recently, a different variety has been introduced with a cone-shaped nib that allows the pen to be held at an angle, giving more freedom of movement and making sketching easier.

I made this detailed study of a knot with a technical pen. Hatched and cross-hatched lines were used for the shadows, and the fine, linear quality of this type of pen was ideal for drawing the individual fibres of the rope.

Q30 How do I draw with a brush pen?

A | **Brush pens are a relatively new graphic tool.** They are spirit-based with a nylon-fibre, pointed brush tip that keeps its shape. They are available as waterproof or water-soluble in an enormous range of colours, including 22 greys. The colours are fresh and make a good alternative to colour pencils when sketching outdoors.

Brush pens produce a wonderfully smooth, free line that is easy to use for making quick sketches or gestural drawings (see Question 43). They are suited to a wide range of subjects, from figure studies to landscapes.

The fluid lines of the brush pen are ideal for a quick sketch using loose, gestural marks. This figure was captured with a simple outline, and her skirt and hair were drawn with scribbled shading.

Project

MATERIALS: Brown waterproof pen, rough watercolour paper,
coloured brush pens: green, dark green, brown, terracotta

Brush pens are suited to quick sketches on location. The smooth, fluid lines can be used to describe and simplify the main elements of the composition, and by combining a simple palette of two or three colours you can achieve the effect of a finished drawing in a matter of minutes.

1 Use a waterproof pen to make a quick, schematic impression of the landscape using fluid lines and dots to mark the position of the horizon, the tree and the lane. Simple, flowing lines are very descriptive for recording the shapes and contours of the landscape.

2 With a water-soluble brush pen in green, fill in the detail over the top of the brown pen marks. Use the pen to add solid marks and loose shading. Use a damp brush or a wetted finger to dilute the ink to give a lighter tone that can be spread and blended on the paper.

Loose, fluid marks describe the foliage of the tree

3 Using a darker green water soluble brush pen, add further details to add depth and tone across the image. Use a variety of lines, dots and dashes to describe the details on the tree and the grasses growing at the edge of the lane.

Q31 What is silverpoint drawing?

A **Silverpoint is the use of silver wire as a drawing instrument.** Before the advent of the graphite pencil in the seventeenth century, silver wire was used to make marks on paper – Leonardo Da Vinci used this method for some of his early invention drawings. Silver wire gives a smooth, fluid grey line and is very easy to draw with. However, the marks cannot be erased or corrected and will gradually tarnish in time to a brown colour.

You can purchase a special clutch pencil that holds the silver wire, or alternatively push the wire into a piece of wooden dowelling. The wire is available in different gauges from thick to thin. Before drawing you will need to prepare your surface with a thin coating of zinc white gouache; the silverpoint will glide over the surface. There are prepared, primed papers also available specifically for silverpoint drawing.

Lead solder, gold and platinum can also be used to draw with, and the marks will not tarnish.

This silverpoint study of a sheep's skull illustrates the fine detail that can be achieved and the subtlety of the marks.

Q32 What is scraperboard drawing?

A | Also known as scratchboard, this is a drawing technique that uses a board coated with a china clay surface which can be scraped away using specialist tools to reveal the white underneath. The boards are available as either black with a white undercoat, or white onto which you can draw with Indian ink. The ink must be allowed to dry before scraping away. You can achieve crisp, clear lines with an overall effect of a woodcut or engraving. Once you have finished scraping you can add coloured inks to the drawing to give it an added dimension.

There are several tools available that will result in different marks: a diamond shaped one gives broad marks, and a trowel-like tool can be used to scoop out. Do not scrape too deeply as the board is relatively thin, and it is advisable to mount it onto a thicker board before you start work.

I applied thin washes of water-soluble ink onto this scraperboard drawing of a dock scene.

For this drawing I first drew the trees' shapes onto white board using black ink. When dry, I scraped into the ink to draw the pattern of the tree trunk.

Project

MATERIALS   Black scraperboard, white Conté pencil, scraper tool, Indian ink, brush

Select a subject with high contrast of light and shade – a sunlit scene
with strong shadows is ideal.

1 Sketch the main elements of your composition onto the scraperboard with a white Conté pencil, which can be corrected. Bear in mind that you will be scraping away the areas of white. Look for the negative shapes to define the subject. Establish the position of the horizon.

2 Start to scratch away the board surface, using the Conté marks as a guide. Use short horizontal and vertical strokes to describe the fronds of the palm tree. Scrape away larger areas to represent the negative shapes in between the branches. Gently blow any dust off the drawing.

3 Using the side of the scraper, scratch away large areas of sky with long, broad strokes. I felt that the palm trees were slightly misshapen, so I painted over the white marks with black Indian ink. Once the ink has dried you can scrape it away to rework the area.

4 Start to work on the foreground. Use straight, controlled lines for a lighter tone on the sea on the lefthand side. Draw the sea wall by following the perspective lines (see Question 60) with the scraper tool. The pattern of the path is drawn with lines at different angles.

5 Leave areas of shadow as black, drawing around them with the scraper tool. Knock back the black solid areas in the foreground with short hatching lines. This creates a midtone that adds to the feeling of depth.

6 Work over the image, adding finer details and correcting with Indian ink where necessary, then reworking once the ink is dry.

The negative spaces between the palm fronds help to define their shapes

Follow the direction of any perspective lines with the scraper tool, to enhance the feeling of depth

Q33 What is sgraffito?

A│ The term 'sgraffito' originates from the Italian word meaning 'scratched', and is often associated with oil painting techniques, where the paint is scraped away to give rough lines on the canvas. A sense of texture can be added to a drawing by using a sharp craft knife or pointed instrument to scrape away marks to reveal the paper or an undercolour beneath.

A very hard, smooth hot-pressed paper or Bristol board will take sgraffito marks without over-damaging the surface. Oil pastel is particularly suited to this technique, where colours are built on top of each other and you can scrape away the top layer to reveal a different colour beneath. This technique gives added depth and texture to your drawing, and would be suitable for detailed studies of grass or reeds, or for delineating a model's hair or folds of material.

A scalpel or craft knife can be used on oil pastel to produce different thicknesses of line. Use the tip for fine lines and the edge for thicker strokes. Always scrape away from your body.

In this oil pastel drawing of a boat I used sgraffito to describe the texture of the fishing nets.

Q34 Can I draw with mixed media?

A| Mixing media, using more than one medium in a drawing or painting, can be a wonderful opportunity to experiment and express yourself. For example, a charcoal drawing can be given added depth and richness by applying a watercolour wash. Other combinations that give exciting effects are using a 'resist' technique by combining wax crayons or oil pastels with overlays of water-based ink, or an acrylic underpainting with a pen line and soft pastels with ink. There are many more combinations that will expand your drawing repertoire.

This portrait study was rendered with a combination of gouache and sanguine pencil.

This sketch was made on location using a fountain pen, pastel pen, gouache and watercolour.

Q35 Can I use collage?

A| Collage is the use of a flat surface to arrange an assemblage of paper, found printed ephemera, such as old bus tickets or wine labels, tissue, cloth and other materials such as shells or buttons to create an image. You can easily combine drawing with collage, and it is often suited to a more abstract approach. Transparent tissue overlaid on existing drawings is a simple but effective way of adding a different dimension. Use PVA glue as an adhesive.

This collage drawing grew from a quick fountain pen sketch of a head on a piece of newspaper. I then combined this with other scraps of paper, newspaper cuttings, corrugated paper and sheets of adhesive stickers onto a thick board in an abstract arrangement.

This pen sketch was made on a piece of newspaper

Q36 How do I convey depth?

A | The term 'depth' can be applied to a subject conveying distance, or as a description of form and solidity. Linear perspective (see Question 60) is a drawing principle that is used to convey distance, but it is possible to convey depth in a number of other ways. Tone (see Question 20) is a very descriptive way of adding depth; vary the density of your pencil lines or marks with darker, stronger lines in the foreground and lighter lines in the distance. Depth can also be shown with diminishing contour lines or by narrowing the shape of an object into the distance – a principle known as foreshortening. This can be applied to a figure – for example an outstretched arm pointing toward the viewer will narrow as it recedes. Similarly, you can add a sense of three-dimensionality to a still life drawing by the use of foreshortening; a thin object placed on a diagonal will become narrower toward the background.

In landscape drawings, the principles of aerial perspective (see Question 65) give a convincing sense of depth and distance. Use tone, contrasts of colour temperature and texture, and recession to suggest depth.

This street scene uses the principles of linear perspective to convey the feeling of distance. The downward slope of the rooftops and the way that the lane narrows toward a point in the background, all add to the sense of depth.

This drawing uses tone, texture and recession to suggest depth. The foreground tree is detailed compared to the paler, softer forms of the bushes in the background, which are also smaller in scale.

This drawing of a reclining figure uses the principle of foreshortening to give a feeling of depth.

The torso looks shorter than is natural due to the effect of foreshortening

The leg appears to become narrower and shorter as it recedes toward the background

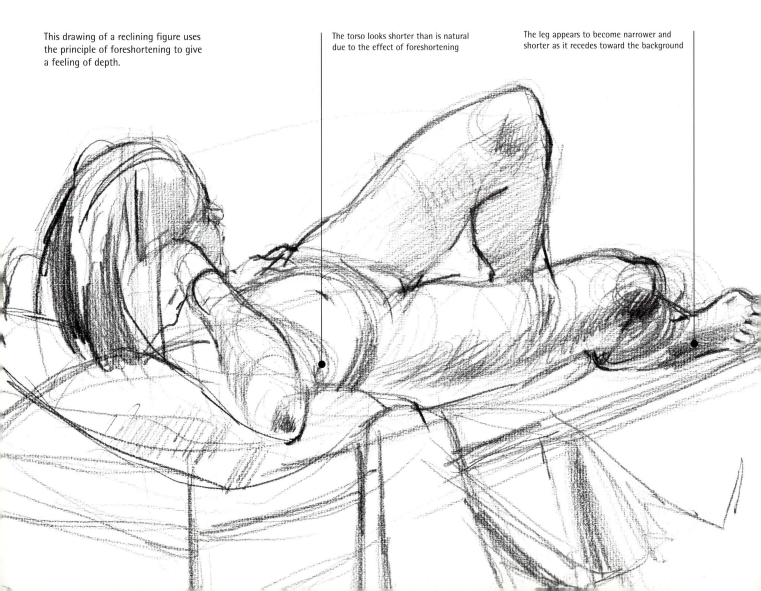

Q37 How do I convey form?

A | **Form, or volume, is defined as 'solid content', and we analyze objects as being either linear or toned.** When drawing you are recording a three-dimensional object on a one-dimensional surface, and there are several ways of suggesting form to imply three dimensions. Light and shade are good indicators of form – what may appear to be a flat shape if rendered in a single tone will take on volume with the use of tones and highlights to describe the form (see Question 20). For example, a round apple may appear as a circle without tone and shading, but by adding a darker tone for the shadowed side and a highlight where the light hits the apple, you will quickly give a sense of solidity.

You can employ several drawing techniques to convey form, depending on your media. For pens and pencils use loose hatching combined with finer cross-hatching and vary the pressure of the pencil marks to achieve lighter or darker tones; in coloured media, such as Conté pencils and pastels, you can add lighter highlights; in charcoal drawing use an eraser to lift out highlights and add lighter tones (see Question 22).

These pencil studies of a statue illustrate the simple effect of tonal drawing to describe form, using highlights to describe the shapes.

The shadow area beneath the lips is conveyed with a dark tone

The ridge of the nose was lifted out with an eraser. A darker tone was used for the nostrils, which are further defined by drawing the shape with an eraser

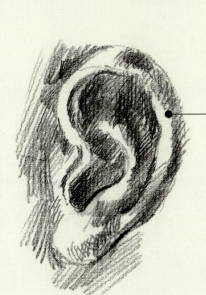

The complex shape of the ear is simply drawn by combining subtle tones and drawing the main shapes with an eraser

The shadow area beneath the eyebrow and to the edge of the nose is conveyed with hatched and cross-hatched lines

Q38 What is loose shading?

A | Shading, or rendering, is the method of showing form and shadow, or the half-tones between light and dark. Loose shading is the free use of your drawing media to achieve form and tone. You can apply the strokes lightly and randomly, or increase the pressure and density of the stroke for a darker mark. Shading can be applied with a wide range of media, such as pencils, coloured pencils, pastel sticks and charcoal. These soft media will move over the paper surface with ease. A pen and ink, however, will not be as free, but you can still apply loose marks with shorter strokes of the pen. Hold the pencil, pen or pastel near the top of the shaft and use a sweeping movement.

The texture of the paper will also determine the type of mark that you make: a rough paper gives a broken line, whereas a smooth paper will produce a clear, solid line.

The loose lines and monotone shades of pencil are particularly well suited to location drawing.

The loose lines and overlaid colours suggest the underlying form of this figure drawing. Long strokes in varying directions reflect the speed at which a drawing can be made with this technique.

Q39 What is controlled shading?

A | **Controlled shading is a method of drawing using a standard line to define form.** Shadows may be rendered, for example, with evenly spaced parallel lines. The shading marks are often made in a diagonal manner. Hold the pen or pencil half way down the shaft for more control. Cross-hatching (see Question 41) can also be a form of controlled shading. This method is suited to pen and ink and technical drawings, or architectural drawings requiring precise detail. Classical drawing teachers used controlled shading for life drawing lessons.

Controlled lines in varying tones describe the shapes and forms of this portrait.

The model's facial features are clearly defined with a few shading marks

The creases and folds of the fabric are captured with regular pencil strokes

Q40 What is contour or outline drawing?

A | **Contour drawing is the use of thick and thin lines or strokes on a drawing to define the shape of an object, without the use of shading or tone.** The lines can be continuous, with some lines running parallel or overlapping to suggest form. This simple and effective drawing method is suited to figure drawing, where a single sensitive line can express a naked figure, clothing folds or muscle tone. The artist Paul Klee once described his method of drawing as 'taking a line for a walk'.

This drawing technique is clearly suited to pens and pencils, but can be rendered in just about any drawing media. A smooth paper will yield a clear, even line, but textured papers may be worth experimenting with for the variety of marks that can be made.

A single line is very effective in describing the human form. This back view was completed with almost a continuous line.

Q41 What is cross-hatching?

A | **Cross-hatching is a drawing technique that is used to express form, texture and shadow.** A series of diagonal, parallel lines overlap each other in different directions, but not always at right angles, as this can appear too mechanical. You can apply the lines in a free manner or with more control. By varying the distance between the lines you can vary the tonal effect – loose, open strokes will give a lighter tone, more densely packed strokes imply a darker tone. This technique is also very effective with coloured pencils: you can overlay different colours to blend colour on the paper and build tone in stages. It is worth practising this technique in different media and on different papers.

This graphic colour pencil sketch illustrates the effect of overlaying hatched lines in different colours. You can 'mix' colours on the paper and build up tones.

Thick lines were used for the darker tone of the background

This dip pen and ink sketch uses very detailed cross-hatching to describe the form of the crumpled paper.

Widely spaced, thinner lines are used to describe the light tone of the shadow

Densely hatched and cross-hatched lines suggest the shadows within the folds of paper

Q42 What is a simple shade drawing?

A | A shade drawing simplifies the image to a degree so that only the shadows appear, thus suggesting the form or shape of the subject. A simple shade drawing is a good discipline for the artist, forcing you to approach the subject without outlines and looking for shapes without detail. This method of drawing works well with very strongly lit subjects with high tonal contrasts. Practise with a bowl, strongly lit from one side. The cast shadow will eliminate the half-tones.

This bowl is given volume and form by the use of shading to describe its shape. The white of the paper forms an integral part of the shape.

This sketch simplifies the scene to a couple of dark tones, suggesting the solidity of the subject.

A few strokes of a brush pen are all that is required to suggest this figure. By changing the direction of the strokes you can imply volume and form.

Q43 What is gestural drawing?

A| The term 'gestural' is associated with the group of American abstract expressionists, such as Jackson Pollock, William De Kooning and Franz Kline, who made violent paint marks on their canvases, expressing mood and feeling and hence overthrowing traditional, realistic painting styles. In a general drawing context the word can mean the free use of marks that interpret the chosen subject, be it figure or landscape, in an uninhibited style. To achieve a gestural drawing you need to relax your arm, wrist and fingers as you draw. Another method is to change your drawing hand from right to left, or left to right, eliminating convention and familiarity to help you to achieve freedom, and loosening your approach.

Charcoal, pastels and pencils are all suitable media for quick, expressive marks. Ink applied with a brush or your finger is also free and descriptive. It is worth experimenting with unfamiliar media and techniques once in a while to refresh your repertoire and extend your drawing style.

This portrait study was made with very free, loose lines, capturing the character of the head.

These horses were captured with a few brushstrokes.

Q44 How do I convey texture and pattern?

A | Every artist has their own individual drawing style and therefore their own personal approach to detail. However, there are techniques to suggest texture and pattern. Their use will be governed to a certain extent by your choice of medium and paper. You can spread ink with your finger to vary the width and density of the line, use 'blobs' or spots of ink to break up areas of your drawing. The spatter technique (see Question 26) is effective for large areas of texture, while a stipple brush is suitable for more controlled marks (see Question 45). The choice of paper is also important: a very rough surface with a soft pencil or pastel gives broken lines and granulation. Wax resist or masking fluid (see Question 27) can also be used to mask out areas and give a slightly uneven texture.

This landscape study was drawn in ink with a fountain pen and brush. I used several different resist techniques to capture the foreground texture of grasses and stone.

Masking fluid was used here to stop out the pattern of the stone wall

The seed heads of the long grass were created with a finger on wet ink

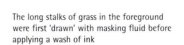

The long stalks of grass in the foreground were first 'drawn' with masking fluid before applying a wash of ink

The rough surface of the stone was created with broad strokes of a candle, before applying a wash of ink

Q45 What is stipple?

Project

MATERIALS   Pale brown coloured pencil, sepia or brown fibre-tip pen, small round stickers, drawing paper

A | Stipple is a drawing or painting technique that uses dots to build up the image. By varying the density and size of the dots you can suggest tone, shadow and form. A drawing produced solely using the stipple technique can be time-consuming and tiring on your eyes, but the results are fresh and vibrant. Pen and ink, technical pens, pencils, and fibre-tip pens can all be used. A stipple brush dipped in ink can be used to give random areas of texture and tone across a drawing.

Hold the pen or pencil at a right angle to the paper so that the tip of the pen touches the surface. You can start a stipple drawing as you would a normal drawing, working freehand if you prefer or following a lightly drawn outline. You can apply random dots to suggest tone and form or follow a regular pattern. Vary the density of the dots to achieve a tonal range, with tightly packed dots for dark tone and more randomly spaced dots for lighter tones.

Stipple is suited to small scale subjects with intricate patterns or details, such as flora and fauna. A large-scale image would be very time-consuming and tiring, but not impossible.

The beautiful symmetry of the pattern on a moth or butterfly's wings lends itself to the stipple technique.

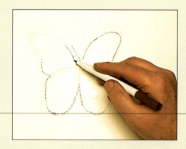

1 Lightly draw the outline of the moth with a pale brown coloured pencil. Place the round stickers on the wings to mask the paper. Using the sepia fibre-tip pen, follow the pencil outline with regularly spaced dots. You can strengthen the line with a double row of dots or by placing the dots closer together.

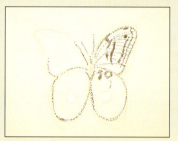

2 Start to add the detailed pattern on the moth's wings. Follow the pattern, describing the undulating lines and circles with rows of dots.

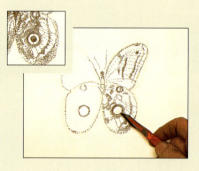

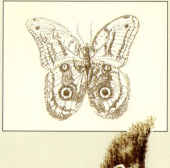

3 Build up the pattern with denser areas of dots to make a more solid tone. The circles on the base of the moth's wings are outlined with a dense colour. Build up the tone around the sticker then remove it carefully with the tip of a craft knife to reveal a white circle beneath. **Inset:** Fill in the centre of the circle with a dense pattern of dots.

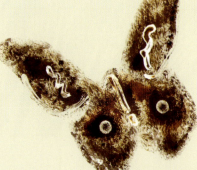

4 Continue to work on the left-hand side of the moth, building up the pattern gradually and using different combinations to describe the detail. Add the moth's abdomen using denser marks on the right-hand side to suggest form.

Variation
A stipple brush (often used for stencilling) can be used to apply ink or paint to a drawing. The effect is much looser and more painterly than that of a pen or pencil. The white patterns were made with masking fluid.

The varying density of the dots was built up to describe the detailed pattern and form of this sunflower.

Q46 What is frottage?

A | Frottage, from the French word *frotter*, 'to rub', is a technique for showing relief design or texture by laying a piece of paper on top of the chosen material, and rubbing with a soft pencil or crayon to transfer the pattern. The range of suitable materials is virtually endless. You can select a natural texture, such as the grain of a piece of wood, or a repetitive pattern, such as corrugated card, depending on your drawing. The pattern can then be integrated into your drawing using different media. You will need a thin paper and a pencil or wax crayon or lithographic pencil for the best results. This is an exciting and addictive technique and will give a fresh, new dimension to your drawings. Your chosen material may dictate the subject matter of your drawing, although it is also suited to a more abstract approach.

The frottage technique was used by some of the Surrealists in France in the 1920s and 1930s. Max Ernst (1891–1976) was one of the artists to find inspiration with this technique, combining several different mediums. He once used the wood grain textures of an hotel floor.

The rubbing of the central section of the straw hat has been incorporated into a larger drawing using other beach materials. I then used a red ballpoint pen to add detail and unify the abstract image.

Project

MATERIALS   Thin paper, black wax pencil, found objects, red ballpoint pen

A combination of materials with a similar theme is very effective in suggesting the subject matter for a drawing made with the frottage technique. Your drawing can be realistic or abstract.

1 You can find suitable materials for frottage on an outing to the beach. Straw hats produce an unusual effect, shells are naturally beautiful with regular patterns, and pieces of driftwood are very versatile.

2 Lay a thin piece of paper over your found object. Here, the central section of the top of a straw hat is being used. Holding the paper in place, lightly rub the wax pencil or lithographic pencil over the surface. The shape and extent of the pattern will be determined by your own personal style and the intended use.

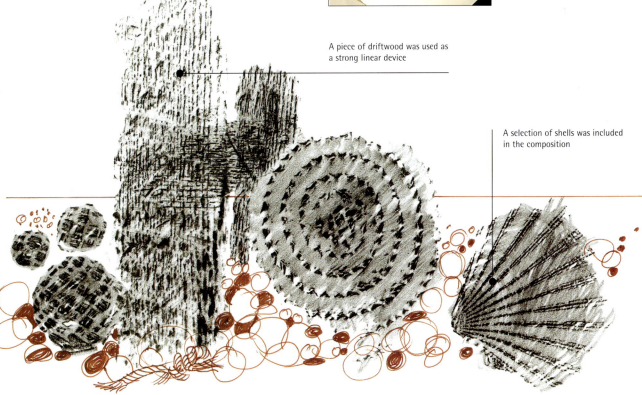

A piece of driftwood was used as a strong linear device

A selection of shells was included in the composition

Q47 What is a linear offset drawing?

Project

MATERIALS   Black etching ink, ink roller, 2 sheets of smooth drawing paper, 9H pencil

A | **This method of linear drawing can be an introduction to simple printmaking.** It uses printer's ink to transfer an image onto a clean piece of paper. Each drawing will be a 'one-off'. Start by sponging or rolling printing ink on to a piece of smooth drawing paper or glass, then carefully place a second piece of paper on top of the ink. Draw on the back of the paper with a hard 'tool', such as the end of a brush or a knitting needle (your marks will not be visible), or with a very hard pencil or ball-point pen. When the paper is lifted off, the image is revealed in reverse. By applying different pressure as you draw you can achieve variation in tone, and a unifying effect is created from the accidental tone of the ink transferred from the undrawn areas. You can also use coloured printing ink.

This technique is suited to still life or figure subjects that can be described with simple contour lines and hatching or cross-hatching for areas of tone.

1 Apply a measure of ink to a palette and load the ink roller. Roll the ink roller across the paper to cover your desired picture area with a solid layer of ink. Do not overink the paper.

2 Place the second piece of paper on top to cover the inked area completely. Press down lightly. With a 9H pencil draw your subject on the top piece of paper. Use linear drawing techniques and contour drawing to describe your subject, hatching for form and add dots or stippling for texture. Try to avoid rubbing your hand across the paper.

3 When your drawing is complete, carefully peel the two sheets of paper apart to reveal the transferred image beneath.

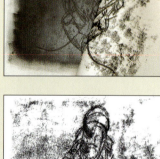

4 The finished drawing shows the clear linear details with a soft background tone where the ink has transferred to the top paper. This accidental tone can be very atmospheric and can give a different dimension to linear drawings.

Variation
In this print, less ink has transferred onto the top paper, giving a subtler, lighter background.

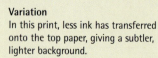

Q48 What is a monoprint drawing?

A | A monoprint is similar to a linear drawing (see Question 47) in that it is a method of drawing or painting that produces a one-off impression print by means of transfer. A monoprint is created by applying oil or printing ink with a brush to the surface of a piece of glass or plastic. The ink can be thinned with white spirit to vary the density of the line or brushstroke. Once the image is complete, place a clean sheet of smooth paper over the ink and press lightly. When the paper is carefully removed, the image will be transferred in reverse.

This method of producing a print is suited to a more expressive, gestural style of drawing (see Question 43) with looser marks and more abstract shapes. Always bear in mind that your image will be reversed and any lettering will appear backwards.

Where the ink was applied in a thin, dilute layer it has started to dry, resulting in soft, textural patterns. Areas of thicker ink have created denser, more solid marks.

Project

MATERIALS   Small piece of plate glass, turpentine or white spirit, brush, smooth drawing paper, oil paint or etching ink: brown, red, yellow

A cockerel's plumes are well-suited to loose brush strokes. This method of printing allows the use of different coloured inks that can be blended on the glass surface to further extend the colour range.

1 Using a palette, dilute the brown paint with turpentine or white spirit until it is slightly thinner. With a brush, draw the shape of the cockerel directly onto the glass. The thicker the paint, the denser the printed mark. A thin layer of paint will start to dry relatively quickly on the glass.

2 Apply the areas of red and yellow to build up the shape of the cockerel and add details such as the comb on its head. Mix the red and brown paint together for the cockerel's chest. Blending can be done on the palette or on the glass. You can remove any mistakes with a cloth dipped in a little white spirit.

3 Carefully place a sheet of smooth paper over the image. Press down lightly over the inked area beneath, taking care not to move the paper or press too hard. Peel the paper back gently.

4 The drawing has been transferred onto the paper in a mirror image of the original. The resulting variation in texture and density is comparable to a lithographic print. A second piece of paper can be applied over the original drawing giving a softer image, as here.

Q49 What is a drawing system?

A | A drawing system, or frame, was a device used in the sixteenth and seventeenth centuries by artists as an aid to the accuracy of a drawing, especially for analyzing the effects of foreshortening and perspective. The subject is viewed through a grid divided into equidistant squares. A grid is then drawn in a sketchbook or onto the prepared drawing surface using the same number of divisions, for example ten across and ten down. The frame is attached to an easel and placed in front of the subject. The artist looks through the frame and plots the image by transferring the position of the subject seen through the grid. The artist's head must remain still and the distance from the frame remain constant in order for the drawing to be accurate.

A homemade frame can be constructed from a stiff piece of card divided equally with thread into a grid. The artist's view through the grid is different from the camera's view in this shot.

The position of the subject, seen through the grid, is then transferred to a grid drawn in a sketchbook or a prepared sheet of paper. Use the grid to plot the position of the key features of the pose. Here, I chose a view slightly to the left of that seen through the camera.

Q50 What is squaring up?

A **Squaring up is a system that allows you to enlarge a sketch to your chosen finished size.** Lightly pencil a grid over your sketch or small drawing using equidistant squares, for example 1 in (2.5 cm) square. Label the squares along the horizontal and vertical sides with letters and numbers in order to plot positions, for example D2. Draw a second grid onto your drawing surface twice or three times the size, or to whatever scale you wish your finished drawing to be.

Plot the lines and marks made on the smaller image onto the larger grid. Keep the lines simple, as you may wish to make small changes to the finished image.

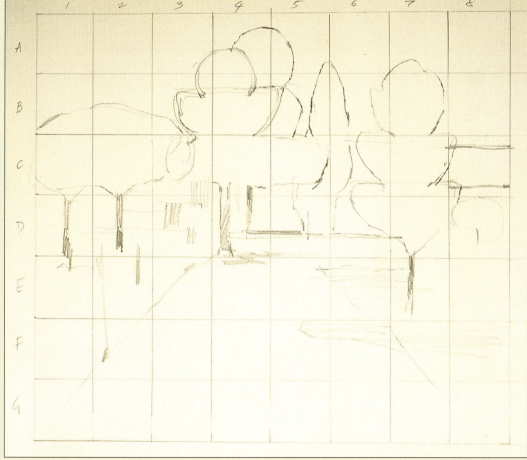

Overlay a 1 in (2.5 cm) grid over your sketch or drawing. Draw a larger 2 in (5 cm) grid to the scale of your finished work and mark off the same number of equal squares. Label the grid. Plot the lines and main elements of your sketch onto the larger grid, using the grid as a map reference.

Q51 How do I work from photographs?

A | **The use of photographs as an artistic aid has often been frowned upon.** However, although they should never replace the sketchbook, they can be a great help to the artist, acting as an *aide-memoire* when time and weather are against you on location, or for recording a particular pose when a model is tired. The camera also has the advantage of capturing the fleeting moments of skies, shadows or figures and animals in motion that even a quick sketch will not achieve with sufficient detail.

With the advent of inexpensive disposable cameras there is no need to purchase expensive equipment. An instant camera will provide you with material for immediate use. Think about using black-and-white film for pictures with contrast and tonal range, suitable for transferring to a charcoal drawing, for example. Digital cameras and computer programs are opening up a different dimension to the artist, but can be equally effective as reference material.

This black-and-white photograph reduces the contrasts of a bright, sunny scene to a range of monochromatic tones.

Taking the photograph as my starting point, I drew this pencil sketch using loose marks for the foreground texture, eliminating the details on the building to simplify the drawing.

The strong shadows cast over the road by the poplar trees caught my eye. Back in the studio I used coloured pencils to capture the light of the sun through the trees.

Q52 What is sighting with a pencil?

A| You can use a pencil as a measuring tool when making representational drawings, to assess the proportions of your subject. In order to measure and compare the proportions, start with a standard measurement. Hold the pencil at arm's length, keeping your arm steady and straight. Close one eye and align the top of the pencil with the top of your chosen subject. Move your thumb down the pencil to record the measurement. You can then compare the length of this measurement to other objects in the composition, thus assessing the size and proportions. For example, the length of one window may fit three times into the height of the building. These measurements, once transferred to your paper, will help in the accuracy of your drawing. You can use this method before you start or as you work.

Hold a pencil at arm's length and take a measurement. Here, the spire can be divided into three equal measurements, as marked on the drawing.

Q53 What is sight sizing?

A| Sight sizing is a measuring method that transfers the size of the object seen by the eye to the same size when drawn on the paper. Imagine a sheet of glass in front of you and that you are tracing your subject onto the glass: the subject will be drawn at sight size. To achieve this when drawing, close one eye and, holding your arm straight, hold up a pencil against your chosen subject so that the top of the pencil aligns with the top of the object. Move your thumb down the pencil to record the total height or width of the object. Then, without moving your thumb, place the pencil on the paper and mark off the measurement. It is important to close one eye – try measuring the same object with both eyes open and the difference will become apparent.

Here, the depth of the hat is measured off at sight size.

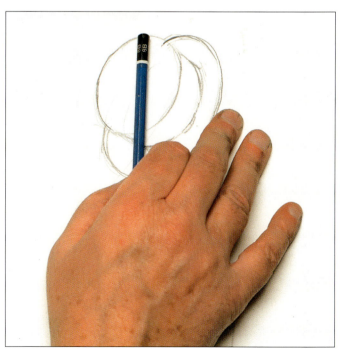

The same measurement is transferred to the drawing.

Chapter 3: Drawing Subjects

You can find inspiration in the grand vista of an open landscape, or in a simple arrangement of flowers. Each subject offers the challenge of selecting the best composition, and choosing the most suitable drawing tool or technique. This chapter offers an overview of the most popular drawing subjects with suggestions on how to approach each one.

Q54 How do I compose a drawing?

A| **Composition comprises balance, rhythm and harmony within a picture.** Spaces, shapes and colours all have a bearing. Much of the pleasure of making a picture comes from the search for harmony. A viewfinder (see Question 14) can be a valuable piece of equipment to help you to decide the crop and format. Make thumbnail sketches (see Question 55) to help you to assess the different elements of the picture – the verticals and horizontals, and the negative spaces in between (see Question 59). Some pictures benefit from an 'L'-shaped composition; the empty space is as important an element as the subject.

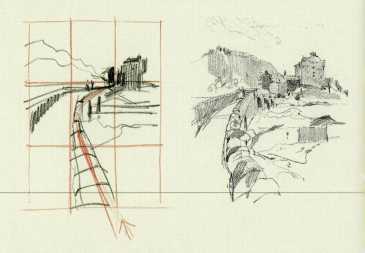

How you organize your composition is obviously a personal choice, but there are some artistic theories that can help. In Classical teaching the Golden Mean or Section was the theory of proportion. This was supposed to express the secret of visual harmony. In simple terms it is the mathematical ratio 8:13. In general, however, the rule of thirds is a simpler guide. Imagine a grid of thirds over your picture, balance can be achieved by placing objects where the horizontal and vertical grid lines intersect. This division also helps with the position of the horizon in landscape drawings – an object placed in the centre of a picture will often jar the visual senses, and the horizon placed at the halfway point looks unnatural. A landscape will have more harmony with two-thirds foreground and one third sky, or vice versa. However, always remember that rules can be broken!

Another compositional device is to use elements of the picture to guide the viewer's eye into the drawing and direct it toward the focal point, known as lead-in lines. For example a road or river in a landscape study, or a long object placed on a diagonal in a still life, will help to direct the eye. You can also use a block of colour or an empty space to this end.

This thumbnail sketch for the finished drawing on the right, illustrates the use of the rule of thirds. The horizon is placed on the top third and the wall, leading the eye into the picture, falls in the central third.

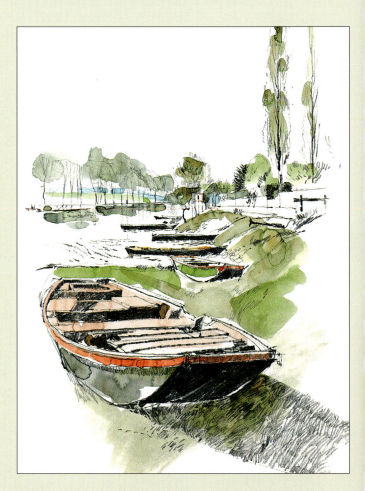

This still life follows a triangular composition, with the jug forming the highest point just off-centre. The rolling pin, placed on the diagonal, acts as a lead-in.

The tall, portrait format for this pencil and wash study enhances the use of diagonals to lead the eye through the picture space. The foreshortened boat in the foreground draws the eye, aided by the flash of red on its prow.

Q55 What is a thumbnail sketch?

A Any small, preliminary drawing can be described as a 'thumbnail' sketch. Such sketches can be made very quickly, in any medium, to assess and simplify a composition before proceeding to a larger finished work. Often the most inventive ideas and pictures have literally come from sketches on the back of an envelope.

Use your sketch to decide on the format, whether portrait or landscape, and to analyze where the main point of interest lies. Loosely draw in the main components, including any areas of shadow that suggest the direction of light. The addition of a line delineating or 'framing' the edges of the image will help you to establish the composition.

You can use any medium for a quick sketch: pencils, ballpoint pens, fibre-tip pens and brush pens all move quickly over the paper. Carry a small sketchbook to record your impressions and thumbnail sketches. You can use your sketch to add notes about colour, to use as reference for more detailed drawings.

Pen and ink is equally suited to making thumbnail sketches as pencil. The fact that you can't correct your marks is an advantage, as your searching lines are important in making a quick response.

Quick, simplified sketches can help to analyze a model's pose.

This quick sketch, using pencil and watercolour wash, simplifies the main elements of the scene.

Q56 How do I decide on the scale of my drawing?

A | The finished size or scale of your drawing depends on several factors: the size of your studio or work space, the paper size and ease of transportation, and, to a certain degree, the subject matter. Consider how you intend to use your finished drawing – whether it is a simple sketch to record shapes and colours, or whether you intend to display and frame it. Your drawing style may suit a particular size support – for example, detailed, fine drawings tend to be smaller in scale than looser, more expressive works. Your chosen medium may also dictate the scale of your drawing; pen and ink tends to suit a smaller scale than charcoal or pastel, for example. You can make the smallest sketch as an *aide-memoire* for a larger, finished work, or a small quick study, of a sleeping cat for instance, may be all that is required. Small drawings can be enlarged by squaring up (see Question 50).

A landscape scene or a skyscape may call for a larger working area, although grand vistas can be recorded with dramatic effect on a smaller scale. A large drawing does not necessarily mean that the whole page must be filled – the spaces that you leave blank are as important as the drawn areas, adding drama to the image. Figure drawings are more suited to a larger working area, and those that focus on a particular area of the body are very effective on a larger scale.

In essence, there is no limit to the size and scale of a piece of work, but, practically, limits have to be set.

A portrait study benefits from a large-scale drawing, giving a sense of presence. I chose to draw this seated figure on a piece of paper sized 22 in x 25 1/2 in (560 mm x 660 mm).

Sometimes landscape features are given more impact by concentrating them on a small scale. This sketch uses minimal shading and tone to record a sunlit building.

Small-scale sketches are very effective in a single media. This pencil sketch uses short strokes and scribbled marks that would be more insubstantial on a larger scale.

Q57 How much detail should I include?

A| The amount of detail you include in a drawing will primarily be guided by your own personal style, but there are other factors to consider, too. Every subject will have some limitations – size and scale, the time available, the type of paper and your chosen media will dictate to a certain degree. For example, if you are drawing a tree in full leaf, how can you include every leaf and twig? A form of shorthand is required, suggesting leaves in some areas and leaving others blank, letting the eye imagine the details. This shorthand can be used for other subjects, such as details on buildings or flowers, or repeated pattern on fabric.

Some media are suited to very detailed drawings, such as pencil, technical pens and pen and ink, and other media, such as charcoal, lend themselves to more abstract styles. A smooth paper is better for detailed drawings as the drawn line is unbroken.

The subject matter of this ink study lent itself to a highly detailed drawing. The cast-iron work and paned windows are all included, drawing the eye through the picture.

Q58 How do I know when my drawing is finished?

A| Someone once said that 'it is not that a drawing is unfinished, but that you stopped at the right time'. It is very easy to overwork a drawing or painting, and the 'less is more' analogy is very relevant in art. Adding every single detail can result in a fussy and confusing picture. Try to suggest areas of detail and leave some spaces blank for the drawing to breathe. Experience will tell you when you think that the drawing has gone far enough – simplicity is the keynote. Try to see simple shapes and shadows, and bear in mind that a lot can be achieved with the minimum amount of work. Often the spontaneity of a rough drawing can have more life than the finished piece.

A light wash suggests the summer sky

Rough lines follow the sweep of the road

This drawing started as a simple pencil study, with loose marks and lines describing the sweep of the road and the railings. A little more detail was added to the building, suggesting the doors and windows. At this stage I could have progressed further, tightening the drawn lines to make the study more realistic. However, I decided to add a light watercolour wash to the sky and trees to complement the loose, open style.

Q59 What are negative shapes?

A | The negative areas of your drawing are the areas in between the positive, drawn subject – the blank spaces between solid shapes or marks. Negative shapes play an important role in contributing to your final image and composition. Much of drawing from life is about looking – whether your subject is a still life, landscape or figure – and in order to assess the shape of the solid object you will need to be aware of the shape of the spaces in between. Negative shapes help you to draw accurately. Winter trees, for example, are a mass of confusing trunks, branches and twigs, but by looking at the shapes of the gaps in between you will be able to simplify the main elements.

Before you start to draw your picture, it is sometimes helpful to make a quick thumbnail sketch of the negative shapes. You will find that searching out these hidden areas will be a great benefit as you progress.

I used different colours to pick out the negative spaces around this chair.

The negative spaces define the shape of the chair, which is left blank

The skeletal structure of a tree trunk is a good subject to practise drawing negative shapes.

Q60 What is one-point linear perspective?

A | Linear perspective is an artistic principle that gives the illusion of three-dimensional space on the flat, two-dimensional surface of your drawing paper. There are two simple guidelines to remember that will help you to achieve the effect: parallel lines appear to converge at a point on the horizon, and objects appear smaller in the distance. Imagine sitting or standing in the centre of a railway track in the desert. In the far distance the tracks will converge at a point on the horizon, known as the vanishing point. The horizon is at your eye level (remember that your eye level will change depending on what height the viewer is). Perspective lines above the horizon will appear to slant down, and those below the horizon will slant up. To help you to draw the angles of the perspective lines correctly, hold your pencil at arm's length and lay it along the railway track, then transfer the slope to your drawing. Alternatively, you can make some cardboard angle scissors (see Question 63) that will help you to measure the angle correctly.

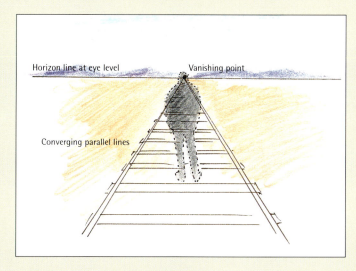

Horizon line at eye level   Vanishing point

Converging parallel lines

Simple linear perspective can be illustrated by a straight road or railway track. Start by drawing the horizon then adding the parallel lines so that they converge at a point on the horizon, known as the vanishing point.

In this pencil and wash study the road follows the principles of linear perspective, narrowing toward the horizon, and the telegraph poles reflect this sense of recession by diminishing in size toward the horizon.

The telegraph poles recede towards the horizon

The edge of the road converges towards the distance

Q61 What are two- and three-point perspective?

A The basic principles of perspective have been explained in Question 60, but different rules apply when looking at an object from an alternative viewpoint. For example, if looking at a rectangular box from above, with the box directly in front of you and the horizontals parallel, the top lines will diminish to a single vanishing point at eye level (see Figure 1). If you change your viewpoint to view the corner of the box, the sides will diminish to two vanishing points at your eye level (see Figure 2) – this is two-point perspective.

Three-point perspective adds another vanishing point and dimension above your eye level. This applies to a situation where you are looking at a tall building from below. A third vanishing point is established where the parallel sides of the building meet at a point above the top of the building (see Figure 3).

When drawing buildings from the side, where you are facing the corner of the building, you will need to be aware of the principles of two-point perspective.

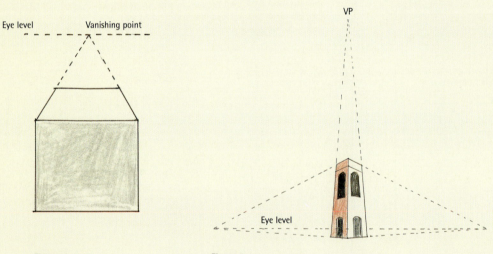

Figure 1
One-point perspective.

Figure 3
Three-point perspective.

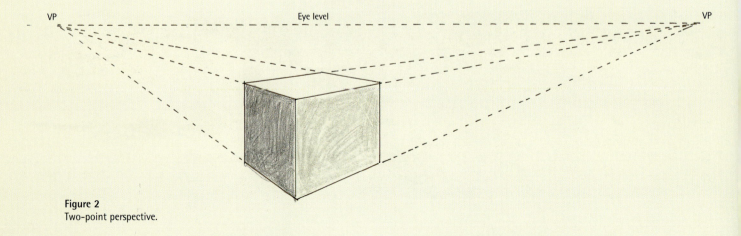

Figure 2
Two-point perspective.

Q62 How do I draw sloping perspective?

A | This is sometimes called accidental perspective and applies to situations where the subject involves uphill or downhill perspective lines. The examples below show how this principle applies to a street scene looking uphill and downhill.

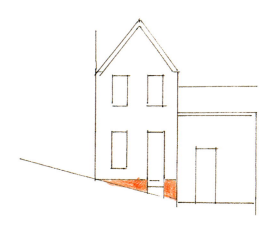

Figure 1
The elevation of a house on a slope. The red wedge shape shows the floor level against the slope of the hill.

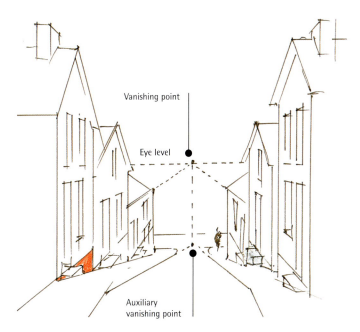

Figure 2
A view looking downhill with the distant eye level governing the angles of roof lines. The accidental viewpoint is below eye level and gives the point where the downhill lines converge.

The gentle uphill slope in this drawing is above the eye level of the artist. To render this convincingly you need to establish an imaginary, or auxiliary vanishing point (see Figure 3).

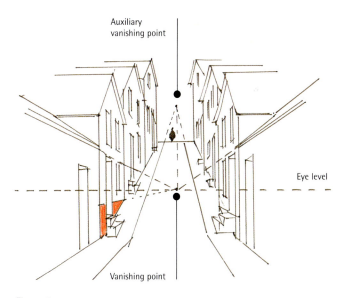

Figure 3
An uphill view – the roofs, windows, doors all vanish to your centre of vision or vanishing point. The accidental vanishing point is directly above the centre of vision, and the sides of the street which are sloping all converge at this imaginary point.

Q63 How do I measure perspective?

A | **The principle of perspective can be accurately measured and drawn using simple mathematical guidelines.** You may wish to practise this method if drawing architectural or interior subjects that require a high degree of accuracy. It is worth practising the technique to familiarize yourself with the characteristics of perspective, and you will then feel more confident at drawing them freehand without recourse to measuring. As with all drawing methods, it is important to look at your subject carefully and record what you see. Perspective rules can be more complex, and further study of specialist books will be required if you wish to investigate in more detail.

To record perspective accurately you need to draw the angles between the lines correctly. The diagram below explains how perpendicular objects, such as telegraph poles, recede toward the horizon. This simple rule of measuring could also be applied to the distance between the sleepers on the railway line, or if drawing a tiled floor.

This complex interior uses the principles of perspective in the ceiling, floor and receding arches.

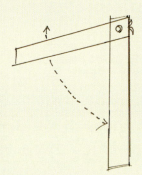

In time, you will be able to judge perspective lines without measuring. Angle scissors are a simple device that can be made at home using two strips of card joined with a split pin. Hold one side on a vertical and move the other along the slope of the line and adjust to measure the angle. Transfer the scissors to your paper and mark off the line.

1 Establish a vanishing point on the horizon. Add the first telegraph pole and measure the distance to the second pole, drawing it in. Draw a line connecting the top of the poles and extend this to the horizon to meet the vanishing point. Repeat adding a line at the base of the poles.

2 Draw diagonal lines between the two poles to find the centre point. Draw a line through the centre point to the vanishing point on the horizon line.

3 Draw a line from the top of the first pole (A) through the second pole where the central line intersects the pole (B) to a point at ground level (C).

4 Raise a vertical line from C to meet the top line at D. This is the accurate measurement for the third pole. Continue to measure the poles towards the horizon.

Q64 How do I draw a circle in perspective?

A Most shapes will distort slightly when drawn in perspective – a circle becomes an ellipse. A simple way of drawing this is to draw a square in perspective (see Figure 1). Add the diagonals of the square to find the centre, then bisect the square horizontally and draw the ellipse to touch the four edges (see Figure 2). The back semicircle will appear smaller than that closer to you. In time you will be able to draw an ellipse freehand and avoid making pointed or blunt ends.

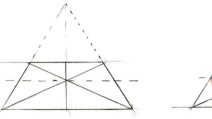

Figure 1

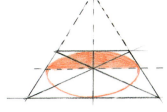

Figure 2

To help you to practise the different shapes that a circular object can make, take a cup or bowl and draw the top at different viewpoints, starting by looking straight on to the side, where only a straight line is visible. Tip the cup towards you and the more circular the shape will become.

This pencil and wash still life includes several different circular shapes. The fruit bowl and ashtray are drawn as ellipses, whereas the orange is given form and solidity through the use of light and shade.

77

Q65 What is aerial perspective?

A | In landscape drawing and painting there are a few artistic principles that help to convey depth and distance where the rules of linear perspective do not apply. By using colour, tone and texture you can add a sense of depth and suggest distance to a landscape. Aerial or atmospheric perspective is an artistic principle that explains the haze of a distant landscape and how to convey this in a drawing or painting. You can convey this effect through colour, tone, texture and scale.

Contrasts of colour temperature are very effective: distant hills appear as cool blues and violets, compared to warmer colours in the foreground. Cool colours will appear to recede and warm colours will advance.

The use of texture and detail will also help to suggest depth. The nearer the object or vegetation, the more emphasis is required for definition. Objects in the distance are softer and more abstract.

Contrasts of tone give a sense of space. Make distant areas paler and graduate tone from dark to light as the objects recede into the distance. This can be achieved by using different grades of pencil (see Question 4) or by varying the pressure and type of pencil marks.

Distance can also be conveyed by scale. Objects in the distance are smaller than those in the foreground. A useful device is to layer clouds, with smaller, paler clouds receding into the distance. This principle also applies to waves in seascapes, where the pattern of the waves becomes smaller in the distance.

Aerial perspective is most noticeable in wide open, panoramic views where distant mountains, hills or fields are seen along the horizon. However, you can apply the principles to any landscape drawing to add a sense of depth and distance.

This distant vista, looking down and across to the fields in the far distance, illustrates the different techniques used to convey aerial perspective. Warm colours and detailed textures appear in the foreground, in contrast to the pale tones and muted shapes of trees and hills in the far distance.

This pencil drawing, made with a range of pencil grades, uses differences in tone to suggest depth.

Q66 How do I convey the effects of light?

A | **Light helps us to see form and understand tonal values.** The fall of light upon an object will create highlights and shadows, and it is these areas that help to suggest the feeling of light.

Establish the source and direction of the light, and keep this consistent throughout your drawing. A figure or object lit from the right will cast shadows on the left. The length and intensity of these shadows will depend on the strength and position of the light. A high light will cast short shadows. This also applies to working outdoors, where the time of day will dictate the length of the shadows – the midday sun casts a short, strong shadow; longer shadows appear in late afternoon with a softer light.

Contrasts of light appear as tones. You can suggest light by making stark contrasts in tone. Make a tonal study of your subject before you, and judge the effect of light (see Question 20). A highlight, indicating where the light hits an object, can be conveyed with white pastel or Conté pencil, or by lifting out pencil or charcoal marks with an eraser. Shadows should follow the shape of the object and, if working in colour, should be a muted colour rather than black.

'Broken colour' is a drawing technique that is particularly suited to suggesting the fall of light across a dappled surface. Leaf shadows or sunlight on water can be suggested by combining dashes of colour with bright highlights.

If working in colour, think about the temperature of the light – is it warm or cool? A sunny day can be conveyed with warm reds and pinks, whereas the light of a cool, rainy day will be blue and grey.

Project

MATERIALS   Drawing paper, coloured pencils in a range of colours

Dappled sunlight is a perfect subject for coloured pencils. By layering and overlaying colours you can create subtle blends and tones on the paper, reflecting the myriad colours of a sunny day.

1 Lightly draw in the main elements of the composition using a pale brown coloured pencil to establish the picture area. Indicate the direction of the light source by placing a few main shadows across the image with a darker brown.

2 Using a light green, loosely shade the top of the trees to suggest the dappled light of the leaf canopy. Use a light blue to overlay the green to give a brighter green on the paper. The broken colour will enhance the feeling of bright sunlight hitting the leaves.

3 Start to work down the picture, adding darker colours where the tree trunks are in shadow. Use solid marks and shading to deepen the tone where the shadow is darkest. Apply a warm yellow to the road and building with loose shading, and start to add details to the barn doors and shutters. The warm colours give the impression of sunshine.

4 Use a blue-grey pencil to follow the pattern of the shadows as they fall across the road. Apply harder marks for the darker tones at the base of the trees where the shadow is darkest, and looser, lighter marks for the tracery of the upper branches. As the shadows recede into the background, use lighter marks to give a sense of depth and distance. Apply violet pencil over the shadows to warm and soften the edges.

Finishing touches of leaf details add texture and depth to the foreground

5 Build the colours in the trees and leaves by overlaying marks from light to dark. Add details to the building and a shadow beneath the eaves. Use a green pencil to suggest the shadows cast by the trees on the grass on the left-hand side of the image. With a blue pencil, add some loose shading to the sky area to enhance the effect of glimpsing sky between the leaves.

Q67 How do I light a subject?

A Professional photographers know the importance of lighting a subject, and it is just as important in drawing, adding volume and drama, particularly for figure and still life subjects. Side, top, frontal and back lighting are all options, preferably from a single light source. In the absence of natural light, daylight or halogen bulbs are available to simulate strong light. Daylight is preferable, but bear in mind that the position and strength of the sun's light will change throughout the day.

Lighting can affect the mood of the subject – a figure lit softly from the side will be subtler, with interesting shadows and tones, compared to a harsh, frontal lit study. Backlighting, or *contre-jour*, throws most of the subject into shadow, almost creating a silhouette. Try different angles of light and make preliminary thumbnail sketches in charcoal to assess the tonal values before you finalize the composition. Look for shadows and highlights that can become an important part of the composition, too.

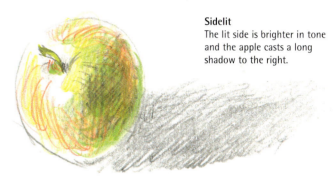

Toplit
A bright highlight appears on the top of the apple, with a short cast shadow beneath

Sidelit
The lit side is brighter in tone and the apple casts a long shadow to the right.

Backlit
Most of the apple's surface is in shadow with only a small highlight. The cast shadow is dark and follows the apple's overall shape.

This quick pencil sketch was made against the light, or *contre-jour*. The subject's features are relatively indistinct and the main element of the composition is the shape of the figure against the bright sunlight glimpsed through the window behind.

To familiarize yourself with the different effects created by varying the light source, draw a simple object, such as an apple or orange, lit from different angles.

Q68 How do I start to draw a landscape?

A | **Painting and sketching outdoors can be a very pleasurable experience, and some of the joy should be in the preliminary search for a subject.** It is all too easy to sit down to draw without some thought of a point of interest. Experiment with a few thumbnail sketches, and try using a viewfinder (see Question 14) to help you to select and eliminate scattered details and finalize the format. Look for broad shapes and a balance across the picture space with one point of interest. A selection of horizontals, vertical and rhythmic shapes all contribute to a pleasing picture. Consider the rule of thirds (see Question 54) and the position of the horizon, for example one third sky and two-thirds ground will concentrate your drawing on the landscape, whereas two-thirds sky and one third ground will transfer the interest to the sky area.

Look for foreground interest and texture: grasses, flowers and hedgerows. Roads, avenues of trees and paths can all be used to lead the eye into the picture area toward a focal point.

These thumbnail sketches illustrate the different effects created by altering your viewpoint to adjust the position of the horizon. The high horizon (above left) gives more emphasis to the foreground, compared to the more central horizon (above right) which changes the balance of the drawing.

This pen and ink drawing uses a landscape format to encapsulate the broad vista. I included the small tree in the foreground to catch the viewer's eye and lead it through the furrows in the field in the middle ground to the buildings in the distance.

Q69 How do I draw trees and leaves?

A | There are many species of trees, and it would be impossible to study them all in detail. However, trees can be generalized into common shapes that will help you to approach them in a more analytical way. By starting with a simple, skeletal outline you can then add detailed tracery of branches and suggestions of leaves.

In winter most deciduous trees will show their 'anatomy', the skeleton exposing the trunks, branches and twigs. In summer it is well worth making a close study of a leaf or a branch in leaf before drawing the whole tree. This will acquaint you with the detail and shape of the leaves. When drawing the whole tree, add leaf details to the lower branches, using a form of shorthand to suggest the leaves over the entire tree rather than attempting to draw each individual leaf. Trees in full summer leaf have three dimensions – volume, light and shade – accentuating large masses, some advancing and some on other planes.

Thomas Gainsborough (1727–88) often used a a piece of broccoli to simulate trees in his studio. Dramatically sidelit, it can look remarkably like a tree in full leaf.

Oak – rounded   Elm – cylindrical   Cypress – columnar

Conifer – conical   Willow – rounded   Cedar - cylindrical

Although leaf structures and masses vary, you can identify a small range of simple shapes in most common trees.

I filled a page in my sketchbook with pencil and wash studies of different trees. Their leaves and gnarled trunks were as interesting a subject as the shapes themselves.

Q70 How do I draw flowers?

A | Great pleasure can be derived in looking for and drawing the intricacies of plant forms. Botanical drawing is a very precise and detailed study, but the artist can use simplified shapes to great effect. Flower heads can be described by geometrical shapes: circles and ellipses for daisylike flowers, bell-shaped cones for daffodils and foxgloves, a tube for an unopened lily, for example. Lightly trace a circle or arc for the extent of the petals before you draw them in detail – you will find that this 'line' will help to maintain the natural symmetry of the open bud. Leaves are composed of curves and often have a central mid-rib from which a tracery of veins extend.

The intense colours of flowers can be captured in a pastel drawing or by using undiluted coloured inks and washes.

The intense colours of lilies can be effectively conveyed with oil pastels. Overlay and blend the pastels on the paper to strengthen the colours further.

This still life of sunflowers and fruit was drawn with a pencil. I then applied a light watercolour wash, using loose marks to suggest the shapes of the petals and leaves, rather than filling in each individual shape.

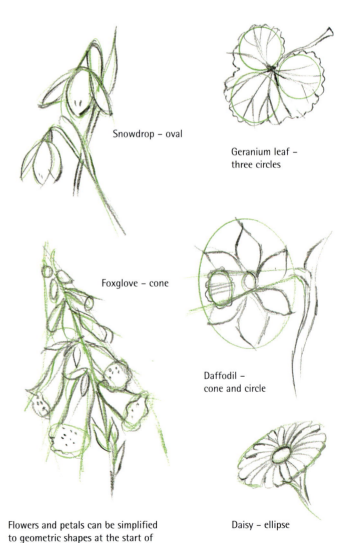

Snowdrop – oval

Geranium leaf – three circles

Foxglove – cone

Daffodil – cone and circle

Daisy – ellipse

Flowers and petals can be simplified to geometric shapes at the start of your drawing. Build up the detail within the overall shape to help keep the natural geometry.

Project

MATERIALS   7B pencil, smooth NOT paper, small brush, concentrated colour inks

A mixed bunch of spring flowers offers a variety of colours and shapes
with which to practise your drawing skills. I used undiluted inks to add the
intense colours of the bouquet, but the drawing is just as effective if left
as a simple pencil study.

1 Using the 7B pencil, start to draw the shapes
of the flowers to establish the composition
and picture area. Use simple circles, ellipses, cones
and ovals to describe the different flower heads.
Add a few petals, again using simplified shapes.

2 Begin to build up the detail on the flowers.
Look for the negative shapes between the
petals and stalks. Count the number of petals and
draw them in, using the outer circle or the ellipse
as a guide to the flower's shape. Find the centre
of the flowers and add the details of the stamens.

3 Continue to add the details of the petals.
Use loose shading to fill in the negative
shapes between the stalks and leaves to define
their outlines and to add a sense of depth. **Inset:**
Use small dots and circles to describe the rounded
shape of the pompom chrysanthemums.

4 Lay the paper flat and wet the petals with a
clean brush. Dip the brush in undiluted ink
and add dots of colour to the flower petals,
allowing the ink to spread a little on the paper.
Use the brush to spread the ink and dilute the
wash to vary the tone of the colour.

5 Continue to add the ink with loose marks
and brushstrokes. The intense colour of the
ink adds a vibrant feel to the drawing and
captures the fresh quality of the spring flowers.

Q71 How do I draw skyscapes?

A| John Constable (1776–1837), the English landscape painter, filled a vast number of sketchbooks with studies of skies. He called it 'skying'. Drawing skies is more of a challenge than painting, where you can use the nature of the paint to create blurred edges and soft colours. For making sky studies you will need a sharp pencil or pen, or a box of coloured pencils.

A skyscape will often include clouds – these are important compositional devices as well as useful for suggesting depth and distance (see Question 65). Clouds are made of vapour and, with a few exceptions, have soft edges. They are ever-changing, so it is necessary to be vigilant and work quickly. Think of a cloud as a three-dimensional shape with a top, side and bottom. Sunlight hits the top of the cloud, making it brighter than the side and underside, which are in shadow.

The principles of aerial perspective (see Question 65) are clearly seen in skies. The cloudless summer sky is always darker directly above, fading towards the horizon. You can convey this in pencil by tonal gradations. You can also use receding clouds in your composition to suggest depth.

When drawing a skyscape you will need to be aware of the time of day and weather conditions. A gloomy, rain-laden sky will have different colour values to a bright, sunny day. Look for shadows on the landscape and also note any shadows cast by clouds. The position of the horizon is an important consideration, too – a low horizon will give the sky dominance in the picture space.

You can employ a number of drawing techniques and media to convey the different cloud types (see opposite). The main cloud types are listed below:

Cirrus – high, wispy clouds

Altocumulus – a mackerel sky, with thin plumes, a sign of fair weather

Cumulus – fair weather, high fluffy clouds with clear patches of sky

Cumulonimbus – towering thunderclouds, fluffy, billowing

Nimbostratus – low rainclouds, ragged in appearance

Stratus – flat grey, layered clouds

Cumulus - white Conté pencil and smudged charcoal

Cumulonimbus - white chalk with smudged charcoal

Cirrus – blue pastel with white gouache applied with a feather

Cirrus – ink wash applied over wax

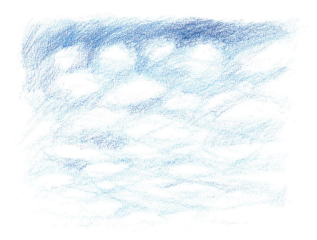

Altocumulus – layers of coloured pencil

Cumulonimbus – pen and ink using cross-hatching

Cumulonimbus – pencil with an eraser to draw the sun's rays

Cumulus – pastel on white paper

Q72 How do I draw seascapes and marine subjects?

A| Artists have always held a romantic fascination with drawing maritime subjects. The sea, boats, piers, the detritus of anchors, nets and ropes, all have appeal. Deckchairs on the beach or pier give unusual, bright colour and pattern to a drawing.

The ever-changing sea has many characteristics, from the soft lapping of a calm, sunny day to raging breakers in a winter storm. Note the effects of recession on gentle waves; make the waves in the distance smaller and closer together and use horizontal marks and dashes. Breaking waves follow a continuous pattern as they roll toward the shore. Use a masking medium applied with a spatter technique (see Question 26) to suggest breaking water and spray before applying an ink wash, or lift off pencil and charcoal marks with a soft eraser.

Pen and ink drawings with a soft wash are a good medium for conveying the soft colours of the sea and coastal sky. Charcoal will give a dramatic effect for a stormy sea, and coloured pencils or fibre-tip pens will capture the colour of a seafront. Sketches of shells and pebbles, made on location or back at home, are suited to pencil studies.

This coloured pencil drawing uses an unusual viewpoint to lead the eye across the bay. The foreground is full of close-up detail of the quayside, ropes and the prows of the fishing boats.

The colours of the striped deckchairs caught my attention for this small sketchbook study in coloured pencil.

The linear nature of piers makes for an interesting and unusual drawing subject. I filled a double page of my sketchbook with this pencil drawing, using a little local colour to pick out details.

Q73 How do I draw reflections in water?

A| **The laws of reflection and refraction (the deflection of objects at an oblique angle) are complex.** It is best to observe closely what you see. If the water is perfectly still, the reflection will be a mirror image, provided that the subject is parallel with the viewer. Ripples, of course, disturb the water surface and fragment the image. Bear in mind the depth of the water, too. A shallow pool or puddle will not only show reflections of the objects surrounding it, but you may be able to see pebbles or vegetation beneath the water surface. The shapes will be refracted. Note also the reflection of the sky on the water surface, and any light that catches the tops of ripples, creating a sparkling effect.

When drawing reflections, blur the edges of the reflected image and use slightly muted colours. Use horizontal marks to draw reflected shapes in rippled water, and mix dashes of the colours of the reflected objects. Use the broken colour technique for coloured pencil or pastel.

This simple pencil sketch illustrates the effects of scale on reflections. The leaning post in the foreground appears taller than the house behind, following the rules of perspective. The post is reflected almost to its full height (leaning in the opposite direction), but the house will show only its top windows.

Dashed pencil marks suggest ripples on the water surface

The reflection in the still water is almost a mirror image of the building

I used watercolour and pencils for this study, smudging and blending them with a brush or wetted finger to convey the soft reflections.

Q74 How do I draw townscapes?

A The commonplace can sometimes be overlooked in art, but there is a fascination in drawing cities and towns, with all the paraphernalia of street furniture, shop fronts, buses, cars and taxis and the hustle and bustle of commuters and shoppers. Industrial areas offer a wide range of interesting subjects – gas works, railway stations and building sites are all worth studying. Markets provide the artist with a wonderful display of colour and pattern.

The busy nature of the townscape lends itself more to quick sketches than to working at an easel, and you may find that this is the best way for you to start your drawing. Sitting outside a café and recording the scene around you can be entertaining. Take notes and make small thumbnail sketches with a pencil, pen and ink or coloured pencils. You will have to work quickly, but the spontaneity of these drawings will have a charm of its own. Brush pens and water-soluble coloured pencils are also good for working on location, and you can achieve a finished drawing with just a few colours in a short space of time.

When drawing townscapes, look for smaller details rather than trying to record a large vista – focus on a single building or a bus stop, for example. To make a larger-scale drawing you will need to have a wider viewpoint, possibly outside the town, and approach the subject as you would a landscape drawing (see Question 68).

This coloured pencil drawing captures the vitality of a busy market.

Cars, buses, trains and everyday transport all move quickly before your eyes. By making studies of toy models you can practise drawing any unfamiliar shapes.

An urban street scene can be quickly recorded with pen and ink.

I chose to use oil pastel for this sketch of an industrial river scene.

Q75 How do I draw architectural details?

A This is a subject that would fill several books. The fascination of looking at buildings can be very rewarding, and the details of all architectural styles and periods make ideal subjects for recording in sketchbooks.

Small details of windows, doorways, brickwork, stone and ironwork all reflect an aspect or period of history. Look up when studying small details – quite often the more unusual and interesting details are above eye level.

A building may offer a wealth of detail. Select the most interesting aspects and record these in note form. You can draw the whole building and use a 'shorthand' to suggest the pattern of brickwork or stones, drawing a few areas in detail and leaving the remaining areas blank. For an accurate rendition you may need to use a measuring method to help you to assess the proportions correctly (see Question 63), and some buildings may require the application of the rules of perspective (see Question 60).

Architectural drawings and details are suited to more linear mediums, such as pencil, pen and ink, and technical pens. A smooth paper will give a clear, fine line. Ballpoint pens and coloured fibre-tip pens are also useful for quick sketches on location.

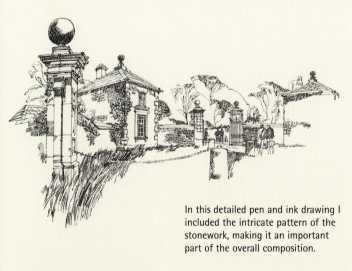

In this detailed pen and ink drawing I included the intricate pattern of the stonework, making it an important part of the overall composition.

Doors make good subjects for detailed studies. Use a pencil or technical pen to draw in the small details, such as the letterbox or the surrounding brick work.

Q76 How do I draw lettering?

A Lettering is all around us, in many languages. Sometimes lettering can be an art form in itself – the stonecarver can make beautiful, lasting lettered monuments on buildings or in the landscape. In our present environment inspiration can be found not only in classical letter forms, but the variety of lettering on shop fronts, doorways and decorative signage, many of which may find their way into your drawing, or become the subject itself.

For carved lettering on buildings of monuments use an outline to describe the letter forms. Signage reversed out on a shop window should be drawn first and then the background filled in around the letters. Lettering on buildings or signs will be affected by perspective – observe the overall shapes and draw what you see.

This pencil drawing includes several different styles of lettering; that on the window is reversed out from the background, while the italic lettering on the right required close observation to keep the letters to the same scale.

Roman numerals can be found on many buildings and monuments, often carved into the stonework. Use shading to imply the shape and depth of the carved letters.

Q77 How do I convey the effects of rain and mist?

A | The drama of a storm, or the subtle shades of rain and mist have inspired many artists. The first challenge is to find a viewpoint, as sitting outside can obviously present problems! It is possible to record rain and mist through the window of your studio or car. You will need to work quickly too, as weather is ever-changing and storm clouds or sharp showers may be closely followed by blue skies and bursts of sunshine.

The effects of a misty or rainy day in an urban setting can also be inspirational, as wet pavements, umbrellas and grey buildings in silhouette suggest a particular mood that can be captured with a simple pencil or charcoal study.

Pencil, charcoal and pastels are all suited to drawing wet weather conditions. The grey quality of graphite gives you a range of misty tones, and charcoal and pastel can be softened and blended to represent blurred edges. Rain can be suggested by long streaks or dashes. Use a soft kneaded eraser to lift off charcoal, pencil and pastel to represent rain or misty clouds. Spattering ink across the drawing (see Question 26) is very effective in suggesting driving rain, or use a more linear technique such as hatching and cross-hatching. A soft ink or watercolour wash is also effective for blurring edges.

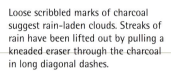

Loose scribbled marks of charcoal suggest rain-laden clouds. Streaks of rain have been lifted out by pulling a kneaded eraser through the charcoal in long diagonal dashes.

Smudged pastel marks blur the edges of the elements of the landscape, suggesting wet and misty weather.

This quick study was made with a pen and water-soluble ink. I applied a light wash over the drawing, softening the lines. I then used sgraffito to draw in the streaks of rain.

I used the sgraffito technique to scrape lines of driving rain across the picture

The distant trees are softened by the wash, causing them to bleed and feather

Q78 How do I convey the effects of snow?

A | **Both snow and frost add a magical quality to the landscape.** Although it may not be practical to sit outside and draw on location, you can take quick sketches or photographs of the scene and work on them in the warmth and comfort of your studio.

On a bright, snowy day all colour seems exaggerated against white, and the contrast appears sharper. You can render this effect in coloured pencils or pastels, leaving the white of the paper to represent the snow or adding white highlights onto a coloured paper. Choose a cool midtone if using a coloured paper and cool coloured pencils or pastels to give the impression of a chilly day. Shadows cast onto snow have a cool blue tinge.

Snowy weather lends itself well to monochrome and tonal studies in pencil or charcoal. Again, use the white of the paper to represent the snow, using negative shapes to define snow-clad bushes, trees and buildings, and lifting off marks to vary the tone and add highlights. Use a kneaded eraser or tortillon to lift off dashes of colour to represent flurries of snowflakes. The introduction of colourful figures – skating or skiing – can bring a winter picture to life.

Frost can throw trees and twigs into relief, creating lacework patterns. You can represent this by drawing the frost-covered twigs with masking fluid, leaving sharp, graphic lines in your drawing once the dried masking fluid is removed (see Question 27).

Project

MATERIALS Grey Ingres paper, Conté pencils, soft pastels

The cool grey paper provides a unifying midtone across the drawing, establishing a chilly feel. A limited palette of colours also helps to keep the image simple and convey the effect of a snow-covered landscape.

1 Using a white Conté pencil, establish the main elements of the composition, placing the horizon line along the top third of the picture area. Add the road leading to the focal point, placed on roughly a third into the picture from the left. Loosely scribble in areas of snow. with the white Conté pencil.

2 To give the impression of a cold, frosty landscape, use a pale blue pastel to add broad strokes of colour to the sky. Use the same colour to suggest the cold shadows cast by the hedge in the foreground.

3 Start to add more details, building on the underlying white and pale blue marks. Use a mid-grey pastel to overlay the shadow on the road with controlled shading, taking the colour to add further details to the building and trees along the horizon. Use a brown Conté pencil to draw the twigs and branches of the bare hedge and distant trees.

4 To enhance the sense of distance, build up the texture of the hedge in the foreground with dots and dashes of burnt sienna over the hedge. The underlying grey of the paper adds to the cool, chilly feel of the drawing. Carrying the pale blue of the sky into the shadows unifies the image.

The small red van on the horizon draws the eye into the picture area

Broad strokes of white and pale blue suggest a frozen landscape

Q79 How do I draw domestic animals?

A| **We all love our pets and like to paint or draw them for pleasure.** Drawing animals requires patience and keen observation. When not sleeping, they very rarely stay still for long, but you will notice that their movements and stances are often repeated – cats in particular will resume a pose in a similar way. Fill your sketchbook with quick, unfinished studies. Constant observation and sketching will improve your visual memory and familiarize you with particular poses so that you will be able to complete a more finished drawing in time.

It is well worth acquiring a basic knowledge of the anatomy of animals. There are many books available for further study, or visit a natural history museum to draw skeletons.

Those media suited to quick sketches, such as a pencil, pen and ink, graphic brush pens and ballpoint pens are ideal for drawing cats and dogs. Use a fluid line, following the outline of the pose (see Question 40), and use contour lines to suggest a haunch or the curve of the ribcage. A wet nose can be suggested with a simple highlight and whiskers loosely drawn or lifted out with a tortillon. If drawing in charcoal or pastel, you can soften the edges and smudge and blend colours to suggest different thicknesses of fur.

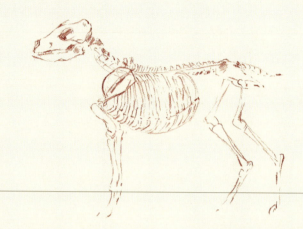

A simple skeletal drawing can help you to understand the underlying shapes and proportions of an animal.

This group of drawings of one dog filled a page of my sketchbook.

A back view gives you the opportunity to use the spine as a guiding line. Quick outline drawing establishes the shape, and loose, scribbled marks suggest form.

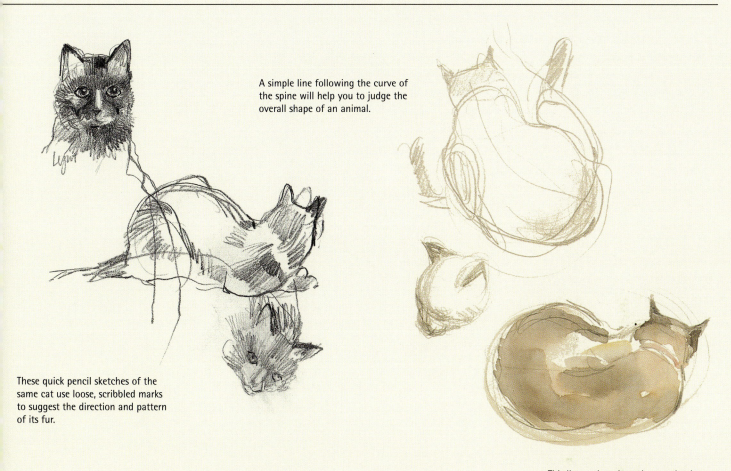

A simple line following the curve of the spine will help you to judge the overall shape of an animal.

These quick pencil sketches of the same cat use loose, scribbled marks to suggest the direction and pattern of its fur.

This line and wash study uses simple shapes to convey the rounded curves of a sleeping cat.

A heavy, smudged line follows the curve of the body, suggesting form.

Lines and simple oval shapes help to delineate the underlying structures of the spine, ribcage and pelvis.

Q80 How do I draw farm animals?

A As with both wild and domestic animals, farm animals are **always on the move.** Watch and observe their different poses, making notes of those that they tend to resume time after time. Start with simple shapes – for example, cattle are based on squares and triangles: the head is wedge-shaped from every angle. Pigs are rounded ovals with pointed ears and tails. Lambs and sheep also have wedge-shaped heads, with their eyes on the side of the skull. Fully-grown sheep, before shearing, have rounded sculptural shapes with fine-textured wool and small, delicate legs. Practise drawing these simple shapes before progressing to a detailed study. Plastic toy models can be used to help you familiarize yourself with animals from every angle.

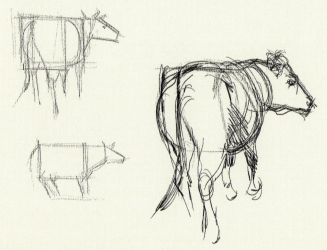

A simple cow shape combines an oblong body with a square, wedge-shaped head.

These pencil studies were made on location. Use the opportunity to familiarize yourself with general shapes so that you can draw the animals with increasing confidence.

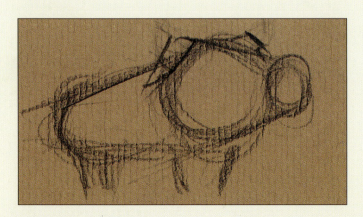

The three-quarter view of pigs and boars can be drawn in the form of a cylinder, with a cone-shaped head. The legs are simply tapered.

Studies of the skeleton and skulls of any animal will help you to understand its structures and proportions.

Q81 How do I draw wild animals?

A For many of us the wild animals that we see are in the zoo, and a visit can be a wonderful place in which to fill a **sketchbook.** The problem with drawing all animals is that most don't stay still long enough for a detailed study. Before drawing, just observe the way the animal moves or rests, and make some quick sketches and notes. Most animals will resume a similar position after a while. If you are on safari, it is worth taking photographs to record movement and using them to compose a drawing when back in the studio.

Wild animals often have interesting markings or fur, or leathery skin. Your choice of medium may be determined by the need for a quick sketch, or by colour notes. Pencils and coloured pencils make a good choice for capturing a quick pose. Soft media such as pastels and charcoal can be smudged and blended to give the impression of dense fur, and a dip pen or technical pen will give the stark, graphic quality more suited to a tougher skin, such as that of an elephant or crocodile.

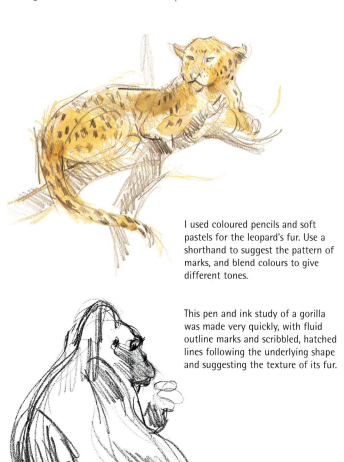

I used coloured pencils and soft pastels for the leopard's fur. Use a shorthand to suggest the pattern of marks, and blend colours to give different tones.

This pen and ink study of a gorilla was made very quickly, with fluid outline marks and scribbled, hatched lines following the underlying shape and suggesting the texture of its fur.

Rather than draw the whole animal, it is often worth making studies of just one feature, such as the head or tail.

Q82 How do I draw horses?

A | **To draw horses it is a great help to have at least a basic knowledge of their anatomy.** Drawing the skeleton and surface muscles will help to explain how they walk, run and jump.

There are various gaits in horses movements: walking, trotting, cantering and galloping. In each, the feet and legs move in differing ways, touching the ground at alternate intervals. Sometimes when galloping, all four feet can be momentarily off the ground. Take a sketchbook to the races or show-jumping or just drawing horses grazing can be rewarding.

The head is worth separate study. Viewed from the front, a rather macabre analogy is that the shape resembles a coffin, or perhaps two triangles with their apexes removed and joined at about eye level.

You may come across horses in a variety of situations. I made this quick sketch while on holiday in Morocco.

Practise drawing horses using a toy model.

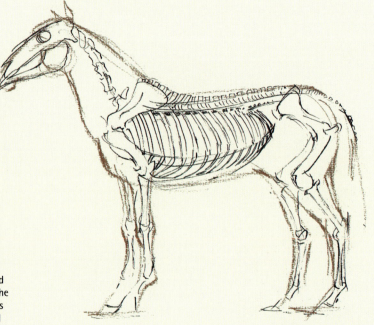

Viewed from the side, the head still resembles a triangular shape. A circle helps to establish the shape of the top of the jaw.

A horse's head resembles a coffin shape. Start with two triangles, joined at the base. Remove the apexes for the muzzle and top of the head. The eyes are placed along the central line and the ears to the side of the head.

The skeletal structure of the horse reveals a sturdy framework. It is worth studying the limbs, as their proportions and the way that they work together are integral to any study of a moving horse.

These quick sketches show the different positions of the legs and feet when the horse is moving.

Q83 How do I draw birds?

A | The range of this subject is enormous, and a detailed study of anatomy would be required for specialist drawings. However, sketching birds is rewarding and takes practice. It is worth taking time to observe and gather information, perhaps drawing the humble pigeons in the park. The owl is also a good bird with which to start. as it remains remarkably still when at rest. Owls are rarely seen in the wild, but a visit to a wildlife centre or bird sanctuary will be of benefit. You can also study majestic eagles, vultures and hawks. A bird table is a good place to record common garden birds, and busy, scurrying farmyard hens are immensely enjoyable with their triangular shapes and variety of colours. The delicate structure of a wing or feather makes ideal material for a detailed study.

These studies of birds of prey were made quickly while on location. I simplified the shapes of the bodies and wings, capturing the pose with a few simple lines.

For these coloured pencil sketches of pigeons I added smudged colour to blend the soft tones of the feathers.

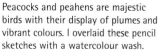

Peacocks and peahens are majestic birds with their display of plumes and vibrant colours. I overlaid these pencil sketches with a watercolour wash.

Q84 How do I compose a still life?

A| As with any composition, a sense of harmony and balance is important (see Question 54). Set up the still life with care, avoiding a 'hole' in the middle of the group of objects. Choose some verticals and some horizontals, perhaps counter-balanced with a round or a patterned object. Choose objects with diverse shapes too – bottles, bowls of fruit or vegetables are a good starting place. The kitchen cupboard or garden toolshed are also worth exploring. Once the group is set up, use a viewfinder (see Question 14) to choose an angle and format, and make a few preparatory thumbnail sketches.

Composition has been defined as 'harmony', order and concord, but 'tension' can be achieved by objects pressing against each other or not fitting neatly within the picture area. Empty spaces are just as important as the drawn areas. Scattered objects will lead to confusion and disharmony.

This pencil sketch is a preliminary drawing to the finished image below, showing a different arrangement.

The warm colour of the onion brings this area forward

The artichoke is placed on a diagonal, leading the eye through the picture

In the finished pencil and wash drawing the main elements of the picture are placed just off-centre in a triangular pattern.

This sequence of thumbnail sketches illustrates the many compositions that can be achieved with the same objects.

The play of light, shadows and the empty spaces are all important elements in the chosen preliminary sketch.

Q85 How do I draw metallic objects?

A | The key to drawing highly polished metallic objects is to note the highlights and reflections dancing across the shiny surface. The shadows and reflections will be tones of black and white or colour. A curved shiny object will show convex reflections echoing the object's shape. Metal objects are opaque and different metals are made up of different colours – steel objects are cooler and bluer than the greys of silver, for example.

There are many metal objects in the home with which to practise, such as saucepans, kettles, soup ladles and cutlery. Study them to observe how light and reflections assume different shapes on the different surfaces. Drawing the reflections in a car is also a good exercise (see right).

Pencil, charcoal, pastel and pen and ink are particularly suited to drawing metallic objects. You can lift off colour with a soft kneaded eraser from pencil or charcoal drawings to add highlights, or use cross-hatching to describe the form of the object with pen and ink studies.

A car is a good subject on which to practise drawing the reflections and patterns in a metallic surface.

This colour pencil study includes metallic objects that are both shiny and dull, calling for different drawing techniques. The warm surface of the rusty kettle is made up of many different tones, with few bright white highlights, compared to the shiny reflections from the chrome cafetière and lamp.

Warm, soft tones make up the flat surface of a rusty iron kettle

The bright white of the paper is left to represent the edge of the chrome handle

The shiny, polished surface of the lamp face shows the reflection of the window panes, distorted over the convex shape

Q86 How do I draw glass objects?

A | Drawing glass is a challenge and is better suited to soft mediums such as pencil and charcoal, where highlights can be lifted out to help to describe the form of the object. With clear glass objects you can make use of the background colours overlaid with a simple outline to describe the shape of the object. A glass containing liquid will reflect other objects around it, and dark bottles will show surface reflections that will be distorted to follow the curve of the bottle. A glass jug filled with flowers will show broken shapes, some magnified, where the stems break at the water level.

As with all drawing and painting, it is important to observe what is actually there, rather than draw what you think should be there. Look for negative shapes (see Question 59) in between glass objects to help to describe their shape, and don't forget to render any cast shadows, as these also help to establish the position and solidity of the object.

Project

MATERIALS   8B pencil, soft and hard pastels, Conté pencils, grey-blue Ingres paper

A plain background is a good idea when drawing glass objects – it will help you to define the negative shapes more easily and avoid any distractions or complications in the composition.

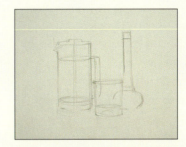

1 Roughly pencil in the outlines of the composition. Use loose lines to follow the contours of the shapes, keeping any shading to a minimum. Use an ellipse to describe the tops and bases of the tumbler and cafetière.

2 Use a blue pastel as a background colour to define the shape of the glass objects. Apply loose, broad strokes to lay a broad area of colour around and behind the cafetière and tumbler. Use a darker shade around the outer edges. Add dashes of white to suggest reflections.

3 Using a yellow pastel, add the oil in the tall bottle, using a few strokes of colour to follow the form of the round base. Do not fill in the colour completely. Use the same yellow for the reflections catching in the tumbler and the light thrown out on the left. **Inset:** Use a black pencil for the metal rim and plunger of the cafetière and to add shading to build up the reflections in the jug.

4 With a white Conté pencil add strong highlights where the light directly hits the glass. Follow the rim of the tumbler. Use a light grey pastel on the foreground mixed together with the yellow from the reflected light of the oil bottle.

The background colour uses the negative shapes to give substance to the glass

5 Continue to work on the reflected light in the foreground, checking that the direction of light is consistent. Return to the highlights on the clear glass, strengthening them further if necessary. The background colour uses the negative shapes to give substance to the glass.

The shape of the glass objects is defined by combining both black and white highlights to follow the form of the objects

Q87 How do I draw interiors?

A | **In our own immediate living and working space there are countless subjects to explore.** The living room, kitchen, stairway and even the potting shed can be a source of inspiration. Other interior spaces, such as cathedrals, stately homes, railway stations and museums also offer possible subject matter. Some of the great masters have drawn and painted interior scenes, and a study of the Dutch School of the seventeenth century, such as Vermeer and De Hooch, will reveal subjects of great serenity and design that you may find inspirational.

Once you have selected your subject, decide on the format by making a few thumbnail sketches of the main elements. You may need to measure any proportions and check the perspective (see Question 60) as you work. Consider the lighting – whether you are going to use natural light from a window, or artificial light. The direction of the light will also influence the composition of the image.

Depending on your subject, your interior drawing may have a detailed, architectural feel suited to technical pens and linear media, or be a looser interpretation, of fabrics and drapes for example, that suits the subtle, flowing lines of charcoal and pastels.

This coloured pencil drawing shows a corner of my studio. Quite often the best subjects are close to home.

The potting shed provided the subject matter for this close-up study in pastel. I used a coloured Ingres pastel paper paper to unify the image with a warm midtone.

By cropping in closely the study takes on an almost abstract quality

The straight-on view eliminates the need for perspective

Q88 How do I draw drapery?

A | **The intricate folds of both drapery and clothing respond to the laws of gravity.** Look for the downward pull of the cloth, using strong vertical strokes to emphasize the direction of the fabric. Folds are defined by their shadows. Use the shadow areas to describe the shape of the fold, looking for the negative shapes (see Question 59) between. Use highlights to emphasize the top of the fold where the light hits the fabric. Smooth shapes that resemble the letters 'm' and 'w' often appear in the folds of fabric.

Patterned fabrics can help in assessing the movement and position of folds – look for where the pattern 'breaks' over a fold. It is not necessary to include all the detail of the pattern – draw a few areas in detail leaving the rest to the imagination.

Soft media such as pastels, pencils and charcoal lend themselves to fabric studies, but a technical pen or pen and ink will give a more graphic, linear quality that is equally suited to describing the vertical pulls of folded material.

The 'w' shape created by the fabric folds is a clue to the shapes created by the pull of the blanket over the chair

The soft dent in the cushion is described by following the negative shapes created by the shadows

Project

MATERIALS   Ingres paper, pastels, Conté pencils

A checked blanket loosely thrown over a chair will fall into soft folds. A cushion offers some subtle dents and creases on which to practise drawing fabric. Look for the shadows to help to delineate creases and folds.

1 Using a light black Conté pencil, draw the main elements of the composition. Look for the shapes created by the pull of the fabric, indicating the creases with simple lines and curves. The checked pattern of the throw helps to assess the changes in the folds. Use loose shading to note the shapes of the shadow areas and the soft dents in the cushion.

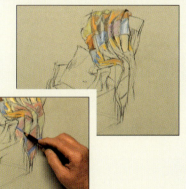

2 Start to roughly indicate the colours of the throw. Add brighter highlights to the top of the folds where the light hits the surface. Use firm marks to give a solid colour to the shapes of the folds and overlay the shadows with black. **Inset:** Work down the drawing, adding the tassels on the edge and using a light orange as a highlight. Apply a loose shading of black over this area to knock back the colours and suggest shadow.

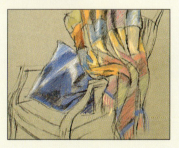

3 Start to work on the cushion. Use a light blue where the corner hits the light and darker tones in the dents and creases. Build the darker tones from light to dark, using the black Conté pencil in the deepest creases. Look for the shapes of dents and follow these to add form to the cushion, adding white or light blue highlights to suggest volume.

4 Work on the throw to add more detail to the pattern and intensify the colours. By applying dark against light you will help to throw forward the folds and creases. Add the shadow of the throw across the top of the chair, reflecting the texture of the fabric.

Q89 How do I measure the proportions of the figure?

A | The human body is a wonderful miracle of engineering, and to start to understand how it works and how it is divided, **we need to know the basics of anatomy.** A simple device to help you to judge the proportions of the body is to use the head. The head height of an average adult will 'fit' 7 to 7.5 times into the body (see Figure 1). For a young child, where the head is quite large and the legs short, the head will fit 4 times into the body. Measure your subject's head with a pencil held at arm's length (see Question 52).

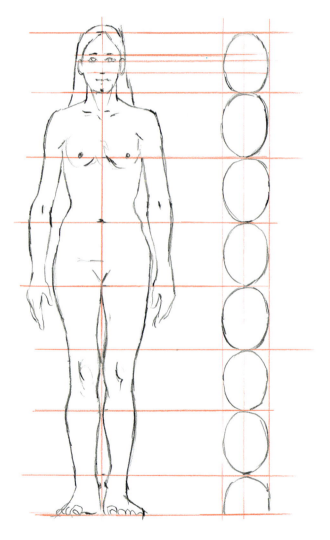

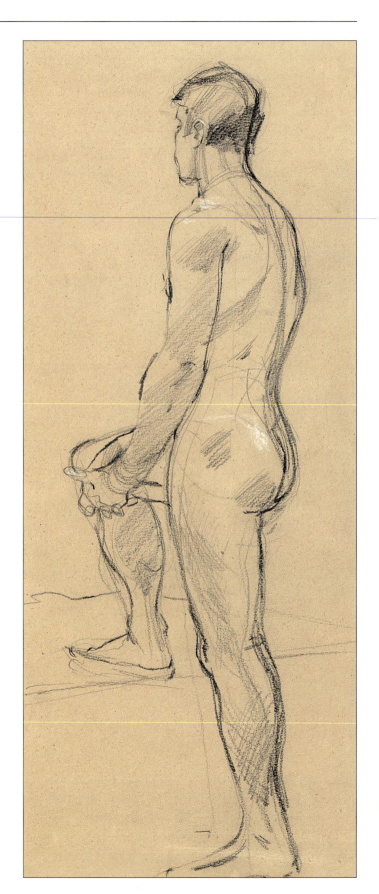

Figure 1
The adult body can be divided into 7–7.5 heads. Note that the body is not equally divided into halves: the lower section, from the hips to the feet is the equivalent to 4.5 heads.

An accurate drawing of the human form hinges on the correct proportions of the figure.

Q90 When do I use a lay figure?

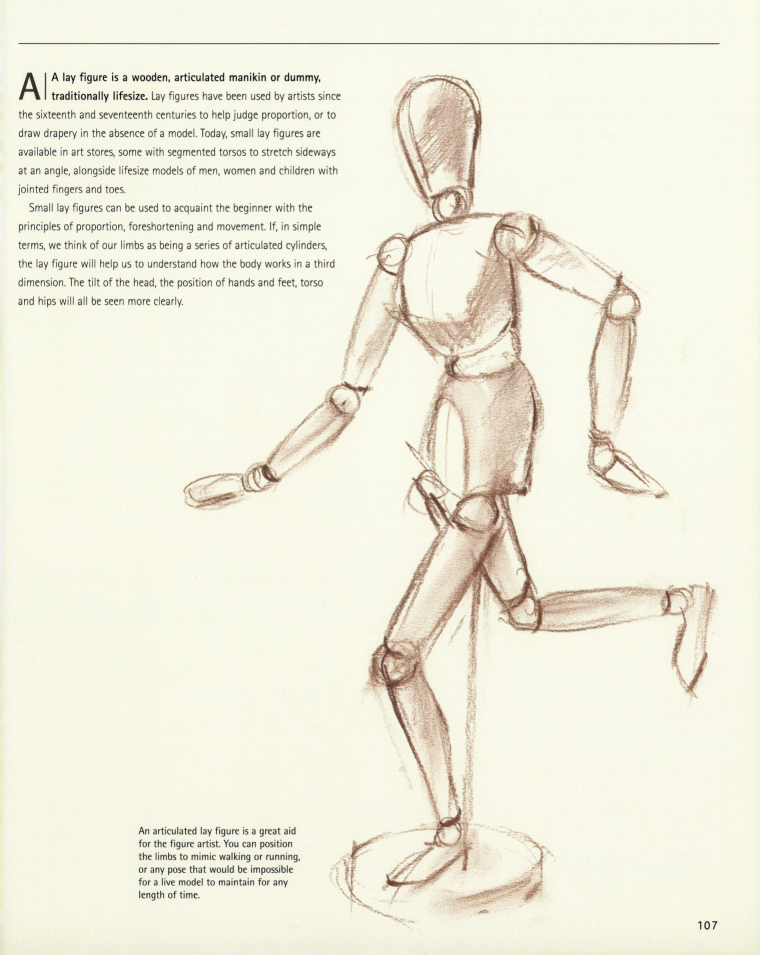

A A **lay figure is a wooden, articulated manikin or dummy, traditionally lifesize.** Lay figures have been used by artists since the sixteenth and seventeenth centuries to help judge proportion, or to draw drapery in the absence of a model. Today, small lay figures are available in art stores, some with segmented torsos to stretch sideways at an angle, alongside lifesize models of men, women and children with jointed fingers and toes.

Small lay figures can be used to acquaint the beginner with the principles of proportion, foreshortening and movement. If, in simple terms, we think of our limbs as being a series of articulated cylinders, the lay figure will help us to understand how the body works in a third dimension. The tilt of the head, the position of hands and feet, torso and hips will all be seen more clearly.

An articulated lay figure is a great aid for the figure artist. You can position the limbs to mimic walking or running, or any pose that would be impossible for a live model to maintain for any length of time.

Q91 How do I draw hands?

Project

MATERIALS   Cream Ingres paper, soft sanguine Conté pencil

A | The most challenging parts of the anatomy to draw are the hands and feet (see opposite); hands in particular can quite easily look like a bunch of bananas! The skeleton of the hand shows that there are a small cluster of bones (the carpels) that join the wrist, and five metacarpels that connect with the fingers and thumb at the knuckles. The fingers have three phalange bones, the thumb two. The palm is roughly bound by five sides.

Practise by drawing your own hand, with or without a mirror, holding an object, clenching a fist or pointing a finger. Start by looking for the basic, simple shapes – it can be a distraction to start drawing every crease or fingernail. Think of the hand and fingers as one, and observe closely how the fingers are often in contact with each other. It is tempting to draw each finger individually, but look at the shapes that are created where two or three fingers touch, not at each finger on its own. Once you have mastered a single hand, try different poses combining the hands with interlocking fingers, or clasping a mug.

It is possible to make a study of your own hand either at rest or holding an object. A soft Conté pencil is an easy medium to work in, but you will need to keep the point sharp by using a fine sandpaper block.

1 Lightly sketch in the position of the fingers around the glass, together with the wrist. Look for an arc created by the spread fingers and note any foreshortening, for example of the index finger.

2 Once you are happy with the outline shape, start to strengthen the lines. Add some loose tonal shading where the fingers touch the glass, and note how the fingers divide into three separate areas, following the underlying joints.

3 Continue to build the tone on the underside of the hand and fingers. Use darker, solid marks for the deeper creases in the palm of the hand, and denser shading where the fingers are flattened on the glass.

4 The shape of the hand is indicated with a variety of tones, using darker tones for the underside of the hand and arm. The final details of the creases on the thumb knuckle and around the fingernail help to bring this area forward.

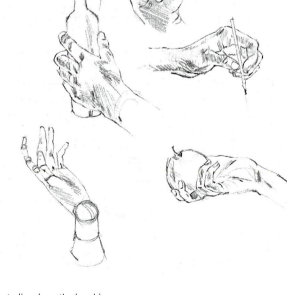

These studies show the hand in a variety of different poses – rarely is each finger viewed separately.

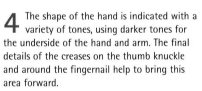

The flat shape of the fingernail helps to indicate the shape of the turned-away finger

The palm and underside of the fingers are rendered in a darker tone

Q92 How do I draw feet?

A | **The feet present a similar challenge to the artist as hands (see opposite).** They take the weight of the body and have a larger and stronger bone structure. In a similar way to hands, the shape of the foot varies with different poses and viewpoints. Seen from the top, with both feet flat on the ground, the top plane slopes out and down to the ground. When seen from the side, this sloping plane on the outer edge of the foot continues down, and the whole side of the foot should be in contact with the ground. In contrast, the inner edge of the foot is raised away from the ground by the arch of the instep. The instep rises from the heel back down to the ball of the foot. In a similar way to fingers, observe the overall shape of the toes. The 'knuckles' create a raised ridge that follows the curve of the toes.

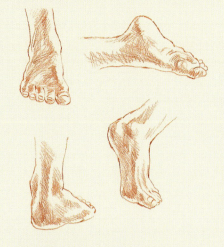

These pencil studies show the surprising range of positions and shapes that the feet can assume.

This sequence of drawings illustrates the outer appearance of the foot and the corresponding skeletal structure.

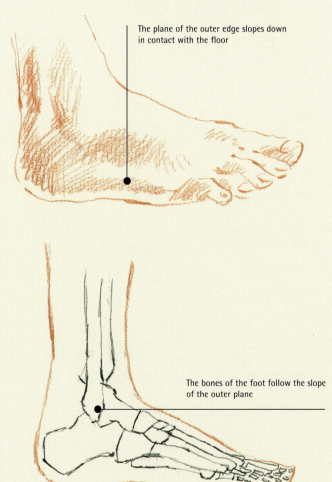

The plane of the outer edge slopes down in contact with the floor

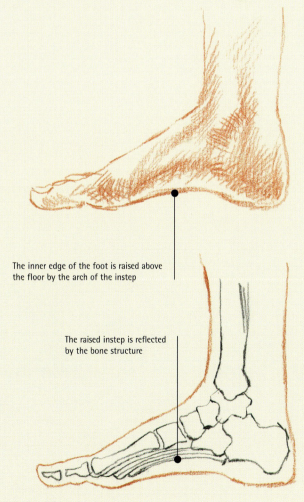

The inner edge of the foot is raised above the floor by the arch of the instep

The raised instep is reflected by the bone structure

The bones of the foot follow the slope of the outer plane

Q93 How do I compose a figure drawing?

A | Some simple thumbnail sketches (see Question 55) will help you to decide the placing and spacing of the figure on the page. The light source is also worth consideration. Backlighting (*contre-jour*) can be very dramatic (see Question 67). You can choose between landscape and portrait format. Think about the background using drapery, or some horizontal, vertical or diagonal devices to hold the composition together. For a more abstract approach, focus on just one part of the figure, or extend the drawing so that it breaks the boundaries of the edge of the paper. Consider full-length, three-quarter view, or head and shoulders poses.

If you attend a life drawing class you will notice that poses come naturally to professional models. Take time to select your pose, choosing one that is relaxed and easily held for short periods of time, and easy to resume following a break.

These sketches show diagonal, vertical and horizontal compositions, some full and some part figures.

This full-length reclining figure study uses the horizontal lines of the bench to enclose the figure. The raised leg helps to draw the eye across the picture area.

Compositions including the seated figure are often triangular in shape. There are a great variety of different seated poses, so consider your viewpoint, the angle and direction of the model's head and position of the legs and feet.

A full-length pose is naturally vertical in composition, but you can vary the feel of the image by selecting a back, side or frontal view.

Q94 How do I draw a nude figure?

A | Working from a life model is one of the most rewarding and necessary exercises in learning to draw and paint. An understanding of the proportions of the body (see Question 89) and a background knowledge of the anatomy – the skeleton and main muscle groups – will all be of benefit. If you attend a life class, start with a series of quick sketches to loosen up and familiarize yourself with the subject. The model will need to have regular rest,s and you should be prepared for the pose to alter slightly once resumed.

The nude figure reveals the structure and balance of the human body. You will need to observe closely how the weight is distributed and how the body compensates and supports itself. Look for the pivotal points – the head, the shoulders and pelvis all give vital clues. With both feet flat on the ground the hips and shoulders will remain level with the head centred. If the weight is shifted to one foot the body balances by tilting the pelvis and counter-tilting the shoulders (see Figure 1). The position of the head is critical in establishing balance and proportion and thus for portraying a convincing figure study. A back view will reveal how the spine curves and compensates for the changes in balance.

Pencil, charcoal and pastel are suited to loose, flowing lines to describe the human form. Contour or outline drawing (see Question 40) can capture the main elements of the figure with a sensitive line. Pen and ink is also a good choice for more detailed studies.

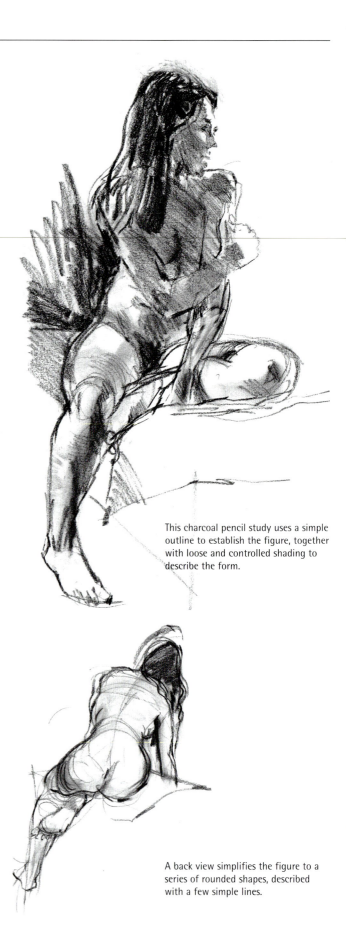

This charcoal pencil study uses a simple outline to establish the figure, together with loose and controlled shading to describe the form.

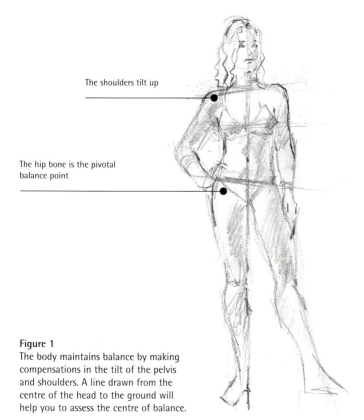

The shoulders tilt up

The hip bone is the pivotal balance point

Figure 1
The body maintains balance by making compensations in the tilt of the pelvis and shoulders. A line drawn from the centre of the head to the ground will help you to assess the centre of balance.

A back view simplifies the figure to a series of rounded shapes, described with a few simple lines.

Q95 How do I draw a clothed figure?

A| In order to draw the clothed figure convincingly, it is a great help to be able to draw the nude figure (see opposite).
The underlying skeletal structure is of course mirrored by the model's clothes. Points of tension need to be studied carefully, and the balance and distribution of weight will be the same as for a nude figure. The pull and folds of fabric (see Question 88) act almost like a second skin but will also respond to gravity, depending on the type of fabric and whether the clothes are tight or loose-fitting. Look for creases in the inner elbow or behind the knees, and folds where the fabric is pulled taut or hanging loose. Think of sleeves and trouser legs as cylinders. All these variations will help to describe the form of the body underneath.

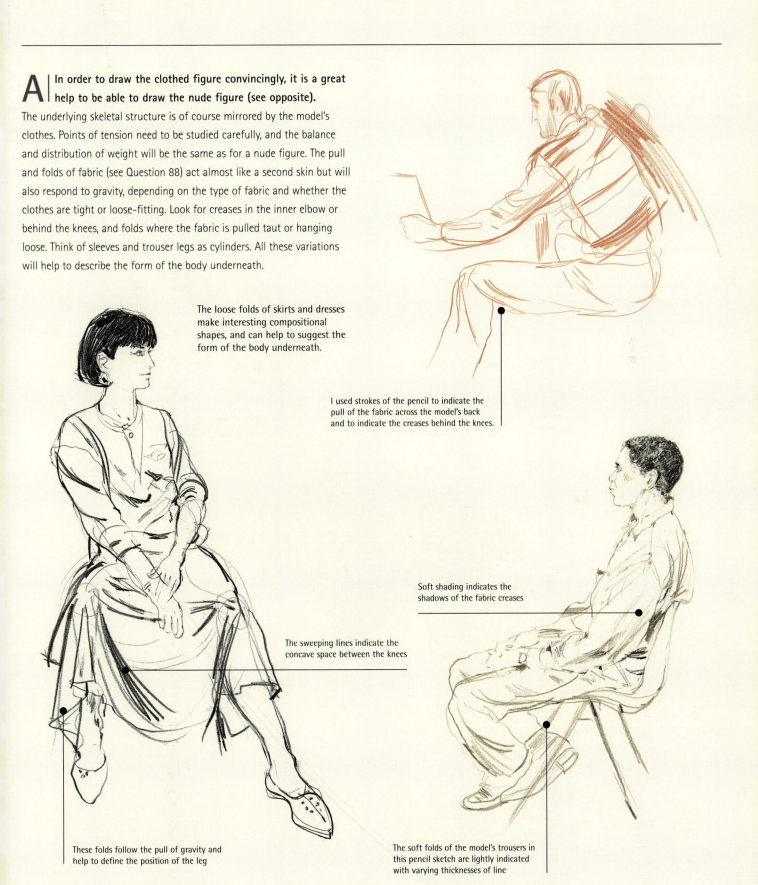

The loose folds of skirts and dresses make interesting compositional shapes, and can help to suggest the form of the body underneath.

I used strokes of the pencil to indicate the pull of the fabric across the model's back and to indicate the creases behind the knees.

Soft shading indicates the shadows of the fabric creases

The sweeping lines indicate the concave space between the knees

These folds follow the pull of gravity and help to define the position of the leg

The soft folds of the model's trousers in this pencil sketch are lightly indicated with varying thicknesses of line

Q96 How do I draw a seated figure?

A **This is one of the most popular poses for figure drawing.** Once a comfortable position has been decided upon, the model can maintain the pose for some time without rest. You can try a variety of different viewpoints – a straight-on, side or back view – and each will present different challenges.

It is important to remember that in any seated pose the chair is an integral part of the composition, forming the support and balance for the figure. Establish the plane of the floor early in your drawing, keeping the chair legs and model's feet consistent. Look for points where the chair and body appear to be 'joined' – along the back, on the arms and seat. These points are key to the balance and support of the figure.

The mass of shapes created by the model's legs, the chair legs, back and arms can appear confusing. Search out the negative shapes (see Question 59) to simplify these elements.

This long, diagonal pose with outstretched legs appears comfortable and relaxed. Although the chair is only lightly sketched, its importance as a support is mirrored by the shape of the model's back and thighs.

The flattened shape of the model's thighs suggest the support of the chair seat underneath

Project

MATERIALS Fountain pen, black ink, drawing paper

When drawing a seated figure, think of the model and the chair as one entity. The spine of a nude figure will reveal how the body compensates for the different distribution of weight, whereas the creases and folds of a clothed figure will help to assess the different tensions created across the body.

1 Lightly sketch in the rough proportions of the figure. Use the bookcase as a measure – the head to waist is equal to waist to knee and knee to foot. Establish the floor plane by ensuring that the sitter's foot is on the same level as the chair legs. Use light lines to establish the angle of the hanging foot and the trouser cuff.

2 Start to add details of the folds of the clothes; these help to reinforce the position of the seated figure. Use hatching on the leg, following the direction of fabric tension from knee to thigh. Use long strokes to follow the form of the shadow areas in the trouser creases. **Inset:** Continue to build the tones and shadow on the trousers, using hatching and cross-hatching.

The shadow of the chair along the sitter's back suggests support

The shoe and chair legs rest along the same plane

3 To place the figure in context, add detail to the background bookcase, continuing to work on the figure and chair. Roughly indicate the floorboards beneath the chair to anchor it on the picture plane.

4 The finished figure works in harmony with the chair, the darker tones along the thigh suggesting the support from the seat. The balance of the composition is enhanced by lightly sketching in the background to put the image in context.

Q97 How do I draw portraits?

A|As with all figure drawing, it is essential to have a basic understanding of the skull before starting to draw a portrait. The shape of the head and the balance of the facial features are crucial to achieving a successful portrait. The frontal view of the head can be compared with an egg and, from the side, to an egg and a sphere (see Figure 1).

Once you are confident with the overall shape of the head, observe closely the placement of the facial features. You may be surprised to discover that the eyes, nose and mouth actually occupy a relatively small space in the overall size of the head. The proportions of the head can be roughly divided into three: from the hairline to the eyebrows, the eyebrows to the nose and the nose to the chin, with the mouth halfway between the nose and chin (see Figure 2).

A portrait is, of course, about drawing much more than just a face. Aim to capture something of your model's character; think about the pose, whether full face, side view, head and shoulders or full-length. Consider the clothing and the setting, and whether to include some of the model's favourite possessions. Talk to your sitter as you draw to maintain a lively and animated expression.

Lighting is also an important consideration (see Question 67). A harsh, strong artificial light will reveal any lines and bone structure, whereas soft side lighting will create soft tones and shadows that can become an interesting part of the overall composition.

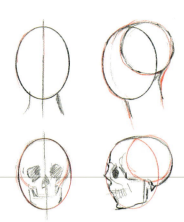

Figure 1
The head can be simplified to an egg shape when viewed from the front. Combine this with a sphere for a side view.

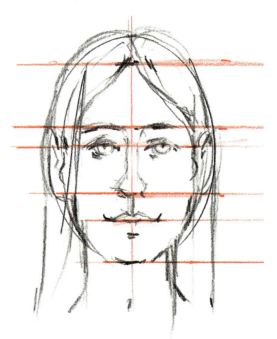

Figure 2
The proportions of the face require careful study for accurate rendition.

The model for this portrait study in sanguine pencil appears relaxed and serene. Talking to your model as you draw helps her or him to maintain a comfortable and natural pose.

Q98 How do I draw a self-portrait?

A | **The most practical way to draw a self-portrait is to look directly into a mirror.** However, you may not achieve an absolute likeness. We all have a left and right side to our face (no one is symmetrical!), our hair may part on one side or perhaps one eye is slightly larger than the other. Your resulting drawing will not be a photographic likeness. It is possible to use two mirrors to correct these inaccuracies (see right). Set the mirrors at an angle so that the first reflection is reversed in the second mirror. This set-up is quite difficult to maintain and requires a lot of concentration and patience. You will need to keep your head very still and return to the same position.

You could use a drawing system (see Question 49) by drawing a grid onto the mirror with a marker pen. You could also work from a photograph, but you may not achieve the spontaneity of a life drawing. Experiment with lighting (see Question 67) to achieve different effects and views, and also consider the setting and whether to include any props in the composition.

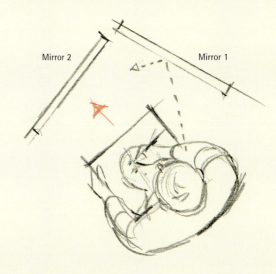

To produce a photographic likeness, set up two mirrors so that your reflection is reversed in the second mirror. Use this reflection as your reference (below).

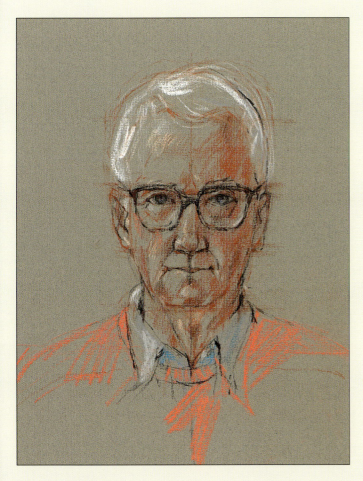

I drew this self-portrait using the method described above.

Q99 How do I draw children?

A| **Children, like animals, are always on the move, and you will need to work quickly.** Start by familiarizing yourself with the proportions of the figure, as these differ greatly from adults. Measure your subject's head with a pencil held at arm's length (see Question 52). For very young children you will find that you will have to make quick sketches or take reference material to work on a more finished drawing. Older children may pose for longer, but keep them occupied with a book or their favourite pastime.

This portrait was drawn with soft pastels on a toned Ingres paper. The simple pose and engaging expression make for a successful, attractive composition.

A one-year-old's head will measure roughly four times into the body. As the child grows the proportion of head to limbs changes. At around eight years old the measure is approximately 6.5 heads. A child attains adult proportions at about the age of 15.

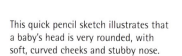

This quick pencil sketch illustrates that a baby's head is very rounded, with soft, curved cheeks and stubby nose.

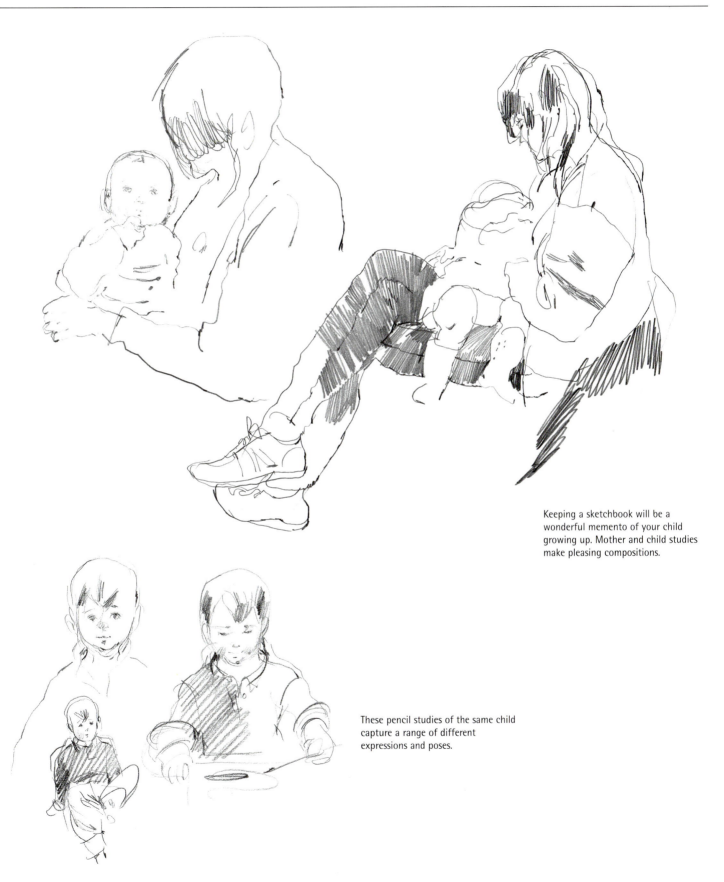

Keeping a sketchbook will be a wonderful memento of your child growing up. Mother and child studies make pleasing compositions.

These pencil studies of the same child capture a range of different expressions and poses.

Q100 How do I draw a figure in motion?

A | **Capturing a fleeting movement in figure drawing needs acute observation and a retentive visual memory.** To help you to analyze the variety of poses you can study a lay figure (see Question 90) – this can reveal the rudiments of running, walking or jumping, but there is no substitute for observing and drawing live, moving figures.

Simple gestures made with a square Conté pastel or charcoal will help capture the essence of the movement. A pen will help to show the lines of a figure moving. Sometimes the tentative marks add a 'nervous' spontaneity. Close your eyes and imagine in a few strokes the way a figure can stretch, leap in the air or hit a ball with a racket, capturing the rhythm of the movement.

The camera, of course, is invaluable at times when there is a need for further finished work. Practise drawing the moving figure to build confidence, and you will be able to draw movement from memory.

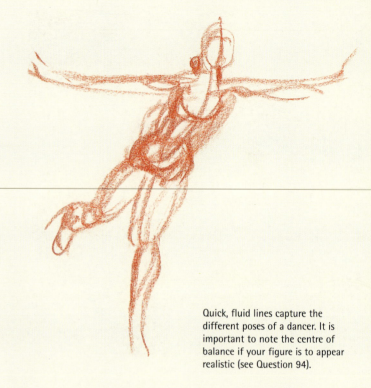

Quick, fluid lines capture the different poses of a dancer. It is important to note the centre of balance if your figure is to appear realistic (see Question 94).

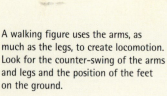

A walking figure uses the arms, as much as the legs, to create locomotion. Look for the counter-swing of the arms and legs and the position of the feet on the ground.

A soft, smudged line describes the
energetic movements of sportsmen.
Search for the dynamics of the pose,
and emphasize these through the use
of line and tone.

Q101 How do I draw groups of figures?

A| Much knowledge can be gleaned by studying the compositions of classical painters; their complex figure subjects were full of geometric formulae. The eye was led to a focal point, often at the apex of a triangular composition, and linear or colour devices helped to lead the viewer around the picture.

Composing a formal group need not necessarily entail these analytical theories. Start by making a few thumbnail sketches to establish a pleasing picture. Consider the lighting and location. Use a combination of seated and standing figures to vary the balance of the composition.

Drawing informal groups of people is much more a random selection of poses, shapes and movements. Observing and sketching is essential in a café or in a park, you will come across groups of standing, sitting, walking and running figures. Don't worry if your subjects move – a sketchbook full of quick notes and observations will be an invaluable source material for further sketches or drawings.

This group of musicians (above) caught my eye and I quickly filled a spread of my sketchbook, adding colour notes for working on when I returned to the studio.

The informal viewpoint for this pencil and chalk sketch includes the back view of a group of figures outside a café. The spontaneity of drawing on location is reflected in the quick, scribbled lines and loose shading.

This preliminary drawing for a formal family portrait includes the group in an interior setting. The direction of the gaze of the figures on the left leads toward the father and child on the right.

Glossary

Aerial perspective – an artistic principle that explains the sense of depth and distance in landscape views where the far distance appears cooler and paler than the foreground.

Aerosol fixative spray – a spray applied to charcoal or pastel drawings to seal the surface and prevent smudging.

Blending – a method of combining colour or tonal marks so that they merge together on the paper.

Broken colour – a technique that can be applied to different coloured media, such as pastels, Conté pencils and coloured pencils, where pure strokes of colour are laid side by side or overlaid to create a layered colour effect.

Cross-hatching – a method of shading where parallel lines are overlaid with diagonal strokes in either a controlled or loose way.

Hatching – a method of shading using strokes of parallel lines.

Linear perspective – a principle of geometry that creates the illusion of three dimensions on the picture surface by the use of converging lines and a vanishing point.

Mixed media – a technique of combining different materials and media in one drawing.

Monochrome – a drawing made in a range of tones of a single colour.

Negative space – the 'empty' space between the solid objects of a composition.

Perspective – a principle that creates the illusion of spatial recession and three dimensions on the flat, two-dimensional paper surface.

Picture plane – an imaginary vertical plane that defines the picture area and corresponds with the surface of the drawing.

Resist – a method that prevents one medium from touching the paper beneath. Ready-prepared resists such as masking fluid are available, or you can utilize the natural repulsion between wax and water, using a candle or wax crayon to draw before applying a wash.

Sgraffito – a technique of creating texture or pattern by scraping away the drawing surface with a sharp blade or pointed tool.

Spattering – a method of creating texture by flicking ink or wash onto the drawing surface to produce spots and speckles.

Stipple – a technique of creating tone and texture with a pattern of dots applied with a pencil or pen.

Support – any paper or material onto which a drawing can be made.

Thumbnail sketch – a quick, small-scale sketch used to assess the different elements of a composition and to help to choose a suitable format for a picture.

Tone – the darkness or lightness of one colour.

Toned ground – the colour of the support that provides a midtone. Can be created by applying a wash of colour or by smudging charcoal or graphite powder on to white paper, or bought as coloured paper.

Vanishing point – the point on the horizon where parallel lines converge following the principles of linear perspective.

Wash – various dilutions of ink or watercolour paint applied to the drawing surface.

Index

Acknowledgements

Author's Acknowledgements With thanks to Roger Bristow for his
original concept, and also to Katie Hardwicke for her patience in editing
and her assistance in collating the material.

Publisher's Acknowledgments With many thanks to Grade Design
Consultants, Ben Wray, Ian Kearey and Margaret Binns.